Media Violence

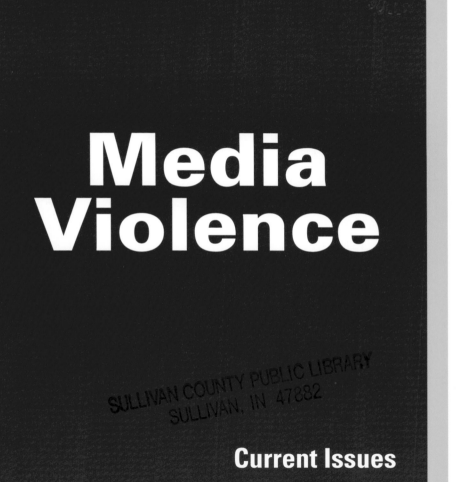

Current Issues

ReferencePoint
Press™

San Diego, CA

Other books in the Compact Research series include:

Drugs

Alcohol
Club Drugs
Cocaine and Crack
Hallucinogens
Heroin
Inhalants
Marijuana
Methamphetamine
Nicotine and Tobacco
Performance-Enhancing Drugs

Current Issues

Biomedical Ethics
The Death Penalty
Energy Alternatives
Free Speech
Global Warming and Climate Change
Gun Control
Illegal Immigration
National Security
Nuclear Weapons and Security
Terrorist Attacks
World Energy Crisis

Media Violence

by Andrea C. Nakaya

Current Issues

ReferencePoint
Press™

San Diego, CA

© 2008 ReferencePoint Press, Inc.

For more information, contact:
ReferencePoint Press, Inc.
PO Box 27779
San Diego, CA 92198
www. ReferencePointPress.com

Picture credits:
Maury Aaseng, 33–36, 49–52, 67–70, 85–88
AP/Wide World Photos, 13, 18

Series design:
Tamia Dowlatabadi

LIBRARY OF CONGRESS CATALOGING-IN-PUBLICATION DATA

Nakaya, Andrea C., 1976–
    Media violence / by Andrea C. Nakaya.
      p. cm. — (Compact research)
    Includes bibliographical references and index.
    ISBN-13: 978-1-60152-035-7 (hardback)
    ISBN-10: 1-60152-035-2 (hardback)
    . Violence in mass media. I. Title.
    P96.V5N35 2008
      303.6—dc22
                                                                    2007031101

Contents

Foreword   6

Media Violence at a Glance   8

Overview   10

How Does Media Violence Affect Society?   21
    Primary Source Quotes   28
    Facts and Illustrations   32

Do Violent Video Games Inspire Violence?   37
    Primary Source Quotes   43
    Facts and Illustrations   48

Is Current Regulation of Media Violence
    Effective?   53
    Primary Source Quotes   61
    Facts and Illustrations   66

How Can the Problems Associated with Media
    Violence Be Reduced?   72
    Primary Source Quotes   79
    Facts and Illustrations   84

Key People and Advocacy Groups   90

Chronology   92

Related Organizations   94

For Further Research   98

Source Notes   101

List of Illustrations   105

Index   106

About the Author   112

Foreword

66 Where is the knowledge we have lost in information? 99

—"The Rock," T.S. Eliot.

As modern civilization continues to evolve, its ability to create, store, distribute, and access information expands exponentially. The explosion of information from all media continues to increase at a phenomenal rate. By 2020 some experts predict the worldwide information base will double every 73 days. While access to diverse sources of information and perspectives is paramount to any democratic society, information alone cannot help people gain knowledge and understanding. Information must be organized and presented clearly and succinctly in order to be understood. The challenge in the digital age becomes not the creation of information, but how best to sort, organize, enhance, and present information.

ReferencePoint Press developed the *Compact Research* series with this challenge of the information age in mind. More than any other subject area today, researching current events can yield vast, diverse, and unqualified information that can be intimidating and overwhelming for even the most advanced and motivated researcher. The *Compact Research* series offers a compact, relevant, intelligent, and conveniently organized collection of information covering a variety of current and controversial topics ranging from illegal immigration to marijuana.

The series focuses on three types of information: objective single-author narratives, opinion-based primary source quotations, and facts and statistics. The clearly written objective narratives provide context and reliable background information. Primary source quotes are carefully selected and cited, exposing the reader to differing points of view. And facts and statistics sections aid the reader in evaluating perspectives. Presenting these key types of information creates a richer, more balanced learning experience.

For better understanding and convenience, the series enhances information by organizing it into narrower topics and adding design features that make it easy for a reader to identify desired content. For example, in *Compact Research: Illegal Immigration*, a chapter covering the economic impact of illegal immigration has an objective narrative explaining the various ways the economy is impacted, a balanced section of numerous primary source quotes on the topic, followed by facts and full-color illustrations to encourage evaluation of contrasting perspectives.

The ancient Roman philosopher Lucius Annaeus Seneca wrote, "It is quality rather than quantity that matters." More than just a collection of content, the *Compact Research* series is simply committed to creating, finding, organizing, and presenting the most relevant and appropriate amount of information on a current topic in a user-friendly style that invites, intrigues, and fosters understanding.

Media Violence
at a Glance

Violent Media Content
Most people agree that media violence is significant. The American Psychiatric Association estimates that by age 18 an American youth will have seen 16,000 simulated murders and 200,000 acts of violence in the media.

Violence on Television
Analysis shows that television content has become increasingly violent—according to the Parents Television Council, the fall 2005 television season was one of the most violent in recent history.

Video Game Violence
Some video games contain extremely violent content, which has raised concern over how this affects children. However, according to the industry rating board, children have many nonviolent games available to them; less than a quarter of the games rated in 2005 were considered too violent for children.

Potential Harms
Numerous studies show a link between exposure to media violence and aggressive behavior. Critics, however, believe that it is impossible to make generalizations from research studies to the real world.

Possible Benefits

Some people believe media violence benefits society by teaching important lessons about life and by letting people harmlessly release violent impulses.

Impact on Children

There is disagreement concerning whether children are particularly susceptible to the effects of media violence. The American Academy of Pediatrics and numerous other public health organizations believe they are, but others insist that children are no more vulnerable than adults.

Parental Regulation

Statistics disagree on the level of parental supervision of children's media consumption. For example, a 2006 report by the National Institute on Media and the Family shows that while only 5 percent of parents say they never talk to their children about the video games they play, 51 percent of children say they never do.

Current Regulation System

In the United States media violence is regulated according to voluntary, industry-established rating systems. Critics charge that these systems do not effectively inform parents or prevent children from accessing violent media content.

Future Regulation

Although violent media content is currently protected by the First Amendment and is not regulated by the government, a 2007 government report suggests that some regulation might be justified in order to protect children from harm.

Overview

In a 2007 report on television violence, the Federal Communications Commission (FCC) finds that the average American household has the television turned on for more than eight hours per day and that children watch between two and four hours every day. "By the time most children begin the third grade, they will have spent the equivalent of three school years in front of the television set,"[1] says the agency. And television is only one form of media. In addition to watching television, both children and adults spend many hours every day using the Internet, watching movies, listening to music, and playing video games. Much of this consumption includes exposure to violent content. Because media violence has such a significant presence in the lives of most people, concern about its effects is widespread. Critics debate how media violence affects society, whether violent video games inspire violence, whether current regulation of media violence is effective, and how the problems associated with media violence can be reduced.

Media in Society

In the United States most people spend a significant portion of their day using numerous types of media including television, movies, video games, music, and the Internet. In 2005 researchers from Ball State University in Indiana released the findings of an extensive study of media use among 400 people. They concluded that the average American spends more time using media devices than any other activity—an average of about nine hours each day. Study participants spent about 30 percent of their time using media exclusively, while another 39 percent of their time was spent using media while also doing another activity, such as watching television while preparing food or listening to the radio while at work. Children's media exposure is also significant. A 2005 study by the Kaiser Family Foundation found that children ages 8 to 18 spend more time in front of computer, television, and game screens than any other activity in their lives except sleeping.

How Much Violence Is in the Media?

Most people believe that the media contain a significant amount of violent content. Says David Walsh, president and founder of the National Institute on Media and the Family, "Depictions of grisly, brutal violence are prevalent in every form of entertainment media, from video games to movies, from pop songs to TV shows."[2] In 2007 the Parents Television Council published an analysis of violence on prime-time broadcast television between 1998 and 2006. The council found that violence increased in every time slot. During the 8 P.M. hour it increased by 45 percent, and it increased by 167 percent during the 10 P.M. hour. "The television season that began in the fall of 2005 was one of the most violent in recent history," it says, "averaging 4.41 instances of violence per hour during prime time."[3] According to the National Institute on Media and the Family, by the time a child is 18 years old, he or she will see approximately 200,000 acts of violence on television, including

> " Because media violence has such a significant presence in the lives of most people, concern about its effects is widespread. "

40,000 murders. Other forms of media also contain significant violence. For example, some of the most popular video games contain violent material, and it is widely available to both children and adults on the Internet. As journalist Rachel Halliburton points out, "It takes no more than a click of a mouse to get through to 'beheading videos, execution images, accident pictures, [and] gruesome scenes' [on the Internet]."[4]

Types of Violence

Violence is portrayed in many different ways by the media. In their book *Violence in the Media*, researchers Cynthia Carter and C. Kay Weaver identify four commonly used categories of media violence: unpunished violence, where the person committing the violence is not punished at the end of the story; painless violence, which does not show the pain, injury, or death that the victim experiences; happy violence, such as that in cartoons where characters are repeatedly hurt and it is portrayed as humorous; and heroic violence, where violence is used by a "good guy" for a positive reason.

> "Most people believe that the media contain a significant amount of violent content."

There is disagreement over whether the different categories of violence have different effects on viewers. For example, some researchers believe that people are more likely to emulate heroic violence or less likely to be critical of happy violence. However, Jonathan L. Freedman, professor of psychology at the University of Toronto, disagrees with the idea that the portrayal of violence is central to its effect, saying, "It is . . . important to note that there is no evidence that any one kind of portrayal of violence, including whether the violence is punished or not, rewarded or not, legitimate or not, has more affect on aggression than another."[5]

Has Media Violence Increased?

Many people believe that both the frequency and the severity of media violence have increased in recent years. They argue that society has gradually become more accepting of violence in the media. British journalist Miriam Gross gives the example of the 2006 James Bond movie

Videos of beheadings can be partially viewed on television and viewed in their entirety online. Children and youth who don't have parental supervision are likely to view these gruesome videos. This is a still from the taped beheading of Nick Berg taken seconds before he was killed.

Casino Royale, which she finds to be extremely violent compared with Bond movies in the past, yet widely viewed by many age groups. Various friends and their children had viewed the movie, she says, and while they had commented on liking it or not liking it, they did not even seem to notice the violent content. "None of my friends had mentioned that the film was full of violent beatings and killings, nor warned me that it contained a scene of horrendous torture," she says. Gross concludes, "Our tolerance of violence . . . certainly seems to have vastly increased. . . . I doubt that such a film would have been open to children under 16 a few years ago. Now they are all rushing to see it."[6]

Reasons for Violence in the Media

There are many reasons for the presence of violence in the media. Some people point out that violence is a fundamental part of human life, so media will necessarily contain it because media reflects reality. Argues Massachusetts Institute of Technology professor Henry Jenkins:

> Media violence is not something that exists outside of a specific cultural and social context. It is not one thing which we can simply eliminate from art and popular culture. . . . Our culture tells lots of different stories about violence for lots of different reasons for lots of different audiences in lots of different contexts. . . . Violence is fundamental to . . . various media because aggression and conflict is a core aspect of human experience.[7]

Other people, such as columnist and editor David Hoppe, contend that media violence is primarily explained by the media's desire for profit:

> Nobody is for murder, beating women or child abuse. But media producers derive big profits by depicting these behaviors, packaging them and making them available, at all hours, via an ever-growing array of delivery systems. They know that as offensive as these images are, there's something in the human animal that wants to look—and that we'll pay for the chance. There's a lot of money to be made in spewing this stuff. Media producers want to make that money as long as they can, they don't want to stop.[8]

> There is disagreement over whether the different categories of violence have differente effects on viewers.

Current Regulation

In the United States media violence is regulated not by the government but by voluntary industry-established rating systems. Movies are rated by the Motion Picture Association of America (MPAA), the trade association of the American film industry. A board rates movies so that parents can decide in advance what is appropriate for their children. All films from MPAA members must be rated, and while independent filmmakers can try to market their movies without having them rated, most theaters are reluctant to screen unrated films.

Television ratings are determined by the individual broadcast and cable networks. The rating system is not applied to documentary and news programming or commercials.

Video games are rated by the Entertainment Software Rating Board (ESRB). Its ratings suggest age appropriateness and also contain content descriptors that indicate elements that may be of concern. Most video game companies use and display the ESRB ratings on their games. There are no laws to prevent children from buying games rated for adults, but many sellers voluntarily refuse to sell adult-rated games to children.

The Recording Industry Association of America provides music recording studios with the tools to label albums that contain explicit lyrics, including explicit descriptions of violence. These

> " **In the United States media violence is regulated not by the government but by voluntary industry-established rating systems.** "

albums are labeled with a "Parental Advisory" sticker, and some stores will not sell albums that carry this label, while others limit their sale to minors. However, the choice of whether the album will receive the Parental Advisory sticker is up to the recording studio and the artist.

Violent Internet content is largely unregulated; however, filters can be used to prevent computer users from accessing it. The Federal Trade Commission, which has conducted a number of studies on the effectiveness of various rating systems, finds that although most media industries comply with voluntary rating systems, they still market their products to children, and enforcement regarding children's access to violent media is ineffective.

Media violence critics point to a vast array of negative effects that have been associated with exposure to violent content. They argue that people who are exposed to a large amount of media violence may be

> **Some people . . . maintain that violence can help teach society important lessons about life or call attention to issues that need to be addressed.**

more aggressive and violent, see violence as an acceptable way to act and to resolve conflict, see the world as a violent place and be afraid of becoming a victim of violence, be less sensitive to violence and those suffering from it, and show antisocial and aggressive behavior. Professor of law Kevin W. Saunders points out that media consumers are exposed to thousands of violent expressions and acts, and, he insists, "It defies common sense . . . to believe that this experience does not have an impact."[9]

Others contend that negative effects of media violence are unproven. Says the Free Expression Policy Project, "No one seriously doubts that the mass media have profound effects on our attitudes and behavior. But the effects vary tremendously, depending on the different ways that media content is presented, and the personality, background, intelligence, and life experience of the viewer."[10]

Benefits of Media Violence

Some people point out that media violence may be positive. Advocates of freedom of expression, such as the American Civil Liberties Union (ACLU), maintain that violence can help teach society important lessons about life or call attention to issues that need to be addressed. For example, says the ACLU, "*Saving Private Ryan* was a powerful movie about the horrors of war, and included many disturbing scenes to illustrate that point."[11] Others argue that media violence is beneficial because it becomes a vicarious outlet for aggression. They point out that people naturally have violent impulses, and argue that by consuming violent media it is possible to release these impulses in a harmless way.

Video Games

Video games are one popular form of media that are often critiqued for their violent content. One area of disagreement is about the exact makeup of the video-game-playing population; however, it is a fact that many different ages and types of people spend many hours playing games. The Entertainment Software Association says that the average video game player in the United States is 33 years old. Others insist that children comprise an important segment of video game players. For example, the National Institute on Media argues that almost half of heavy video game players are aged 6 to 17. In its 2006 report on video game usage, it finds that 42 percent of children play video games for at least one hour per day.

Disagreement also exists over the level of violent content in video games. Critics say games have become increasingly violent. According to a 2004 study by Douglas A. Gentile et al., as many as 89 percent of video games have some violent content and half have significant violent content toward other characters in the game. Adam Thierer, director of the Center for Digital Media Freedom, contends that, "the vast majority of video games sold each year do not contain intense violence." He says, "Of all the games that ESRB reviewed in 2005, less than 13 percent were rated 'Mature' (M) or 'Adults Only' (AO), the categories that contain the sort of violence critics are concerned about."[12]

Whether video game violence causes real world violence is also subject to debate. Some people think it does. For example, the American Academy of Child & Adolescent Psychiatry argues that children who spend a lot of time playing video games are likely to become desensitized to violence, to show aggressive behavior, and to accept violence as a way to handle problems. The National Institute on Media and the Family says, "Scientific research shows that violent video game play increases aggression in young players in the short term. Additional studies show these effects last."[13] Others argue that the scientific evidence does not demonstrate such effects and that video games are unfairly criticized by people who do not fully understand them.

> " **Whether video game violence causes real world violence is . . . subject to debate.** "

Future Regulation

Debate continues over the need to regulate violence in the media. Some people are concerned that children and other vulnerable sections of the

One study found that as many as 89 percent of video games have some violent content and half have significant violent content toward other characters in the game. This boy, who is eight years old, screams as his character is brutally killed during a fight.

population are harmed by media violence and need to be protected by increased regulation. They charge that media producers concerned with profit ignore responsibility for how they are affecting society with their media content. Says Hoppe:

Just as we're finding that the real price of petroleum must include all the costs associated with what it does to our health and the environment, we need to find a way to make the producers of violent media take responsibility for what they're doing to our cultural environment. Violent media is like gasoline: Just because we get off on it doesn't mean it's good for us. We don't need more research to know this; we need common sense.[14]

Others insist that regulating media violence is unnecessary because the media industry does help society make informed decisions about its media consumption. For example, according to Kyle McSlarrow, president of the National Cable & Telecommunications Association, "The industry has dedicated itself to providing customers with easy-to-use tools that both inform parents about TV content and allow them to easily block unwanted programs."[15] In the opinion of the American Civil Liberties Union (ACLU), restrictions on media violence may even be harmful to society. It argues, "Blaming the media does not get us very far, and, to the extent that it diverts the public's attention from the real causes of violence in society, it may do more harm than good."[16]

> " Some people are concerned that children and other vulnerable sections of the population are harmed by media violence and need to be protected. "

The First Amendment

Debates about regulation of media violence often involve the First Amendment to the U.S. Constitution. The First Amendment protects freedom of speech, and free speech advocates like the ACLU insist that violent speech and depictions of violence are included in that protection. The organization argues:

The government cannot limit expression just because any listener, or even the majority of a community, is offended by its content. . . . This means tolerating some works that we might find offensive, insulting, outrageous—or just plain bad. . . . Expression may only be restricted if it will clearly cause direct and imminent harm to an important societal interest . . . [and] only if there is no other way to avert the harm.[17]

The organization insists that there is virtually no evidence that media violence causes direct and imminent harm and says, "If we suppressed material based on the actions of unstable people, no work of fiction or art would be safe from censorship. Serial killer Theodore Bundy collected cheerleading magazines. And the work most often cited by psychopaths as justification for their acts of violence is the Bible."[18]

However, in a 2007 report on media violence the FCC points out that other content-based regulations, such as regulation of indecent media content, have been justified for the purpose of protecting children. It believes that restrictions on violent content may likewise be justified. It says, "Although there are constitutional barriers to directly limiting . . . the distribution of violent television programming . . . [Court] decisions relating to restrictions on the broadcast of indecent content provide possible parallels for regulating violent television content."[19]

Media violence remains a controversial topic with fierce arguments on all sides of the debate. As author W. James Potter points out, "The problem of media violence has been with us for as long as we have had mass media. . . . Despite . . . [great] concern, the problem is still with us today; we are no closer to a solution or even an amelioration."[20] This book offers arguments on both sides of the media violence controversy, exploring the issues of how media violence affects society, whether violent video games inspire violence, if current regulation of media violence is effective, and how the problems associated with media violence can be reduced.

How Does Media Violence Affect Society?

66 **There is strong evidence that exposure to violence in the media can increase aggressive behavior.** 99

—Federal Communications Commission, "Violent Television Programming and Its Impact on Children,"
April 6, 2007. www.fcc.gov.

66 **Drawing a straight line from violence in the media to violence in reality remains difficult if not impossible. The cause-and-effect relationship cannot be reproduced reliably in the lab nor demonstrated plausibly in real life.** 99

—Paul K. McMasters, "The Games Censors Play," *North Country Gazette*, October 19, 2006.
www.northcountrygazette.org.

In the opinion of Paul K. McMasters of the First Amendment Center, "Humans have been grappling for centuries with media demons. The first words uttered were no doubt fearsome to somebody. Then came writing—and worse."[21] As he illustrates, media effects always have been and probably always will be of concern to society. The debate about how violence in the media affects people is continuous. Specific areas of concern are what the existing research shows, whether public opinion on the topic is correct, the various potential harms and benefits of media violence, and its specific effect on children.

Media Effects Theories

Research theories abound about how media content, including violence, might influence people. Two well-known theories are behavioral effects and cultivation. According to behavioral effects theory, people learn about appropriate behavior from the media. Much media violence research is based on this theory. Research is conducted by showing people violent images, then observing their behavior. According to cultivation theory, the media does not cause behavior directly; instead it cultivates certain perceptions, norms, and values. For example, according to cultivation theory, heavy consumers of violent television might assume that the world is more violent than it really is. However, both theories have numerous critics who maintain that they are too simplistic and fail to account for the many complexities of how the media affects people. In the opinion of McMasters, "There is no sure way to predict how media, violent or otherwise, will affect a particular individual."[22] Critics such as McMasters insist that media effects vary greatly depending on personality, life experience, and the intelligence of the viewer as well as the way the media content is presented.

> " Many research studies have been conducted on the effects of media violence with widely differing results. "

Conflicting Interpretations of Existing Research

Many research studies have been conducted on the effects of media violence with widely differing results. Further, interpretations of these results differ. Some people believe the research shows that media violence causes societal harm. For example, in the opinion of the National Institute on Media and the Family, "Since the 1950s, more than 1,000 studies have been done on the effects of violence in television and movies. The majority of these studies conclude that: children who watch significant amounts of television and movie violence are more likely to exhibit aggressive behavior, attitudes and values."[23] The American Medical Association, the American Academy of Pediatrics, the American Psychological Association, the American Academy of Family Physicians, and the

American Academy of Child & Adolescent Psychiatry have all taken the position that media violence harms children.

Others insist that there is no scientific evidence that media violence causes harm. According to Jonathan L. Freedman, professor of psychology at the University of Toronto, "Those who propose that media violence causes aggression have greatly overstated the results of the research, and have generally ignored findings that contradict their views."[24] The Free Expression Policy Project argues that existing research on the effects of media violence is inconclusive. The organization says, "Somewhere between 200 and 300 . . . studies have been done on media violence (not the thousands, as some activists have claimed), and their results are dubious and inconsistent."[25]

Public Perception Versus Research Definitions

Researchers and the general public seem to take different approaches when defining and making conclusions about media violence. For example, in a 2006 study published in the *Journal of Broadcasting and Electronic Media*, the authors found that researchers often count the number of occurrences when measuring violence, so that every occurrence is of equal importance. However, they found that the public is more concerned with the way violence is portrayed—the overall impression—than with the number of violent acts. Members of the public also tend to take a less scientific approach when making conclusions about the effects of media violence. As Potter explains, "Much of what the public thinks it 'knows' about the issue of media violence is based not on factual evidence but on intuitively derived opinions."[26] Many people think that the harms of media violence are obvious and that scientific proof is not required. However, Freedman cautions that such an approach can be dangerous. He says, "Not terribly long ago it was obvious that the earth was flat, that the sun revolved around the moon. . . . Scientific

> " Researchers often count the number of occurrences when measuring violence. . . . However . . . the public is more concerned with the way violence is portrayed. "

research has proven all of these wrong."[27] In Freedman's opinion, "Informed decisions have to be based on the research and conclusions have to be justified in terms of the actual research findings."[28]

Aggression, Violent Behavior, and Desensitization to Violence

There is disagreement over whether exposure to media violence causes harmful changes in people's behavior and attitudes toward violence. Jeff McIntyre of the American Psychological Association says that exposure to media violence increases aggression, desensitizes children to violence, and increases unrealistic fears of becoming a victim of violence. He says, "Just as every cigarette you smoke increases the chances that someday you will get cancer, every exposure to violence increases the chances that, some day, a child will behave more violently than they otherwise would."[29] Potter argues that over time people have become desensitized to much of the violence in the media, and that even as they complain about too much violence in the media, the fact is that there is even more than they realize. "The irony is that most people do not regard the serious assaults and maimings that are portrayed in the media as being violent," he says. "The public has been conditioned to accept a very narrow definition of what is violence—ignoring highly violent acts that are interlaced with humor or that appear in a less-than-real context. People generally underperceive the amount of violence in the media."[30] Filmmaker Shannon Young disagrees with media violence critics about desensitization, insisting instead that violence in the media may actually play a role in sensitizing society. "By not witnessing images of victims are we failing to appreciate the real impact of events or lacking compassion in the wake of suffering?"[31] she asks. She gives the example of footage of Holocaust victims, which helped the world understand the magnitude of this event.

> **People have become desensitized to much of the violence in the media.**

Many people believe that violence in the media has an effect on the way people see the world. Critics say people exposed to media violence are more likely to believe the world is a violent place. For example, according to Healthy Minds, a Web site of the American Psychiatric Association, "Television programs present a narrow view of the world, and the world they present is violent. Thus, people who watch a lot of television are more likely than those who watch less to see the world as being violent and overestimate their chance of being involved in violence."[32] In a 2006 study published in the *Journal of Broadcasting & Electronic Media*, researchers report that the more crime-related television people watch, the more likely they are to misperceive the realities of juvenile crime; for example, believing that it is higher than it really is. However, critics of such

> **Critics say people exposed to media violence are more likely to believe the world is a violent place.**

conclusions argue that people are able to distinguish media portrayals from reality, and that media violence thus does not have a detrimental effect on how people see the world.

Media Violence and the Crime Rate

One common argument related to the effects of media violence concerns the correlation between the amount of violence in the media and the crime rate. Critics maintain that if media violence really does cause violence in society, then the crime rate should have increased along with the amount of violence in the media. However, this has not been the case, so they conclude that media violence must not cause violence in society. For example, Freedman reports that since 1992 the violent crime rate in the United States has dropped dramatically. Yet in that time, television, music, and video game violence has increased. Others, such as Parents Television Council president Tim Winter, disagree, pointing out that there are many other possible factors responsible for a reduced crime rate. He says:

> It is disappointing, in fact pathetic, that some would point to lower national crime rates as "proof" that increased media violence has no impact on children. Given the tens of billions of dollars . . . spent every year on law enforcement, youth-violence intervention, school programs, criminal incarceration, public-service

announcements and the like, it is absurd for such a conclusion to be drawn.[33]

Are Children More Vulnerable than Adults?

Much of the debate over media violence centers on its effect on children. Many people insist that media violence is particularly harmful to children because their brains are still developing and they are still learning about the world. The National Institute on Media and the Family says that young children are more vulnerable than adults to media violence because they are more impressionable, have more difficulty distinguishing between fantasy and reality, and learn by observing and imitating. Potter disagrees with such arguments. Yes, children are vulnerable to media violence, he agrees, but not necessarily more so than other age groups. He says, "People in all age groups are vulnerable, and there is good reason to believe that on many negative effects, older people are even more vulnerable than children. Being an adult does not necessarily mean that one is more highly developed cognitively and can therefore protect oneself better from the influence of media violence."[34]

> " **Many people insist that media violence is particularly harmful to children.** "

Benefits of Media Violence

Some people believe that not only is media violence not harmful, but it is actually beneficial to society. In the opinion of filmmaker Richard Wolstencroft, violence in movies and on television is important because it helps to vicariously release all the potential society has for violence. He also insists that media portrayals of violence help society to question and explain violence. Marjorie Heins, a fellow at the Brennan Center for Justice, argues that even children can benefit from some exposure to media violence:

> Censorship under the guise of child protection has traditionally been, and continues to be, a convenient excuse for not educating children—about media, critical think-

ing, and moral values. We cannot sanitize the world for them, but, through education, we can equip them with the tools to understand and cope with it, including the tools for making smart choices that avoid stupid and vulgar entertainment.[35]

Heins suggests that parents view or listen to violent media with their children and discuss it critically. Joseph P. Viteritti, a research professor of public policy at New York University, agrees. He says, "Sometimes letting the kids watch something and working it through with them is better than not letting them watch at all."[36]

Researchers Cynthia Carter and C. Kay Weaver critique the way that the media violence debate often takes one of two extreme positions—either that media violence is harmful or that it has no impact. Instead, they say, we need to argue a more moderate position. While media violence is not the only cause of social violence, it would be wrong to believe media content has no impact on society. They say, "The media play an increasingly important role in shaping us all both individually and collectively in society. We may not know exactly what types of influence the media have on us, but it is still worth trying to find out how the media might contribute to shaping our perceptions of ourselves and others."[37]

> **Some people believe that . . . media violence . . . is actually beneficial to society.**

Researchers, policy makers, and the general public continue to disagree on exactly how media violence affects society, including what the existing research shows about media violence, whether public opinion on the topic is correct, the various potential harms and benefits of media violence, and its effect on children.

How Does Media Violence Affect Society?

> **"The impact of violent material . . . has been studied for decades. . . . All the major health organizations . . . have signed on to the position that media violence leads to real-world violence."**

—Kevin W. Saunders, "Media Industry Should Take FCC Report Seriously," First Amendment Center, April 27, 2007. www.firstamendmentcenter.org.

Saunders is a professor at Michigan State University College of Law and author of *Saving Our Children from the First Amendment*.

> **"The scientific evidence does not support the hypothesis that exposure to media violence causes people to be aggressive. This was true in 1984 when I published my first review of the literature . . . and it is true now."**

—Jonathan L. Freedman, "No Real Evidence for TV Violence Causing Real Violence," First Amendment Center, April 27, 2007. www.firstamendmentcenter.org.

Freedman is a professor of psychology at the University of Toronto, Canada.

Bracketed quotes indicate conflicting positions.

* Editor's Note: While the definition of a primary source can be narrowly or broadly defined, for the purposes of Compact Research, a primary source consists of: 1) results of original research presented by an organization or researcher; 2) eyewitness accounts of events, personal experience, or work experience; 3) first-person editorials offering pundits' opinions; 4) government officials presenting political plans and/or policies; 5) representatives of organizations presenting testimony or policy.

❝The media do not act alone; they should not be given all the blame for negative effects. But neither should they be ignored; the media are an important factor.❞

—W. James Potter, *The 11 Myths of Media Violence.* Thousand Oaks, CA: Sage, 2003, p. xiii.

Potter is a former editor of the *Journal of Broadcasting & Electronic Media* and author of numerous articles and books.

❝After decades of research and more than a thousand studies, the answer is yes, watching violent content on television affects youth. . . . The evidence is overwhelming that viewing high levels of violent programming increases the likelihood of aggression.❞

—Parents Television Council, "Dying to Entertain: Violence on Prime Time Broadcast Television 1998 to 2006," January 2007. www.parentstv.org.

The Parents Television Council is an organization founded with the goal of preventing children's media exposure to sex, violence, and profanity.

❝Research has not proven that watching violence on television causes watchers to commit violence.❞

—American Civil Liberties Union, "ACLU Comments to the Federal Communications Commission re: MB Docket No. 04-261, the Matter of Violent Television Programming and Its Impact on Children," September 15, 2004. www.aclu.org.

The American Civil Liberties Union was founded to help protect individual rights, including freedom of speech and of the press, in the United States.

❝While the Hollywood contingent may occasionally have something to answer for in their depiction of violence as a problem solving skill, they are certainly not directly responsible for the real causes—our families, our homes, our schools and ourselves.❞

—Shannon Young, "A Dangerous Thing: The Debate over TV Violence," *Australian Screen Education*, Autumn 2004.

Young is a filmmaker.

66The consistent results from these five experiments provide strong evidence that songs with violent lyrics increase aggression-related cognition and affect and that this effect is the result of the violence in the lyrics.99

—Craig A. Anderson, Nicholas L. Carnagey, and Janie Eubanks, "Exposure to Violent Media: The Effects of Songs with Violent Lyrics on Aggressive Thoughts and Feelings," *Journal of Personality and Social Psychology*, vol. 84, 2003, p. 960.

Anderson and Carnagey are researchers at Iowa State University, and Eubanks works at the Texas Department of Human Services.

66There is no direct evidence that music or subliminal messages have directly caused anyone to commit a violent act. [However,] people will undoubtedly continue to make scapegoats of popular musicians for years to come.99

—Courtney Jerk, "Columbine: The Controversy, the Conspiracy . . . the Bullshit," *Shut Up and Listen*, August 7, 2004. www.youbettershutupandlisten.com.

Courtney Jerk is a pseudonym for a contributor to the Web site *Shut Up and Listen*.

66Most people believe that media influences other people and other people's children, but media does not affect them or their own children. This is partially because media effects can be subtle. . . . It's very difficult to convince people that they are influenced by media.99

—David Bickham, interview, "Kids and Viewing TV Violence," *Washington Post*, April 11, 2006. www.washingtonpost.com.

Bickham is a research scientist at the Center on Media and Child Health at Harvard Medical School.

66**There have been four decades of research on the effect of media violence on our kids and it all points to the same conclusion—media violence leads to more aggression, anti-social behavior, and it desensitizes kids to violence.**99

—Hillary Rodham Clinton, interview with GameCore, "Senator Clinton on Violent Games," *CBS News*, August 5, 2005. www.cbsnews.com.

Clinton is a U.S. senator from New York.

66**The depiction of violence in drama is essential for children to understand the world in which they are growing up, both at an individual level and a societal level. Yet the belief that [all] media violence is harmful . . . remains.**99

—Patricia Edgar, "TV Violence: The Good and Bad for Our Children," *The Age*, April 11, 2005. www.theage.com.au.

Edgar is the chairwoman of the World Summit on Media for Children Foundation and founding director of the Australian Children's Television Foundation.

66**There have been instances where criminals or others engaged in violent behavior have imitated specific aspects of a violent movie or TV show. But the fact that millions of other viewers have not engaged in imitation suggests that predisposition is the important factor, and that if the bad actors had not seen that particular movie or show, they would have imitated something else.**99

—Free Expression Policy Project, "Fact Sheet: Media Violence," January 2004. www.fepproject.org.

The Free Expression Policy Project provides research and advocacy on issues concerning free speech and the media. It is opposed to the censorship of any content that does not have a direct, tangible, and demonstrably harmful effect.

Facts and Illustrations

How Does Media Violence Affect Society?

- According to Media Wise, more than **1,000 studies** have been conducted on the effects of violence in television and movies, and the majority show that high exposure to media violence causes aggression in children.

- According to the Free Expression Policy Project, a total of only about **200 to 300 studies** have been conducted on media violence, with inconsistent results.

- In a review of the existing research on media violence, researcher Jonathan L. Freedman finds that only **28 percent** of studies show violence causing aggression, while **55 percent** do not.

- Analysis by the Parents Television Council shows that between 1998 and 2006 violence during the family hour on television **increased by 45.3 percent**.

- An analysis of the content of television commercials reported in *Pediatrics* in 2004 reports that almost **50 percent** of the commercial breaks during sporting events contain at least one commercial showing unsafe behavior or violence.

Violent Crime in the United States Has Decreased

This graph compiled by the Department of Justice shows that violent crime in the United States has decreased since 1993.

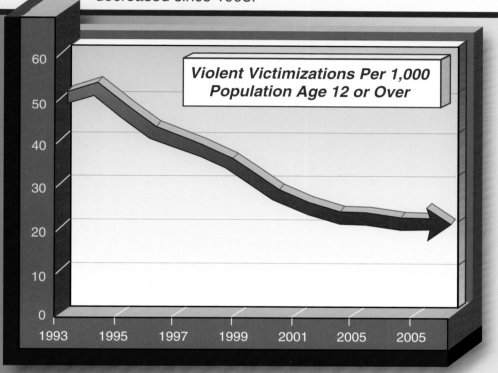

Violent Victimizations Per 1,000 Population Age 12 or Over

Source: U.S. Department of Justice, "Criminal Victimization, 2005," September 2006. www.ojp.usdog.gov.

- The National Youth Violence Prevention Resource Center estimates that nearly **75 percent** of violent scenes on television feature no immediate punishment for, or condemnation of, violence.

- According to the Kaiser Family Foundation, children between **ages 8 and 18 spend more time** in front of computer, television, and game screens than any other activity except sleeping.

Parents Believe Media Violence Harms Children

According to this chart of parental attitudes to media violence, the majority of parents believe that exposure to violent media contributes to violent behavior in children.

How much, if at all, do you think exposure to violence in the media contributes to violent behavior in children?

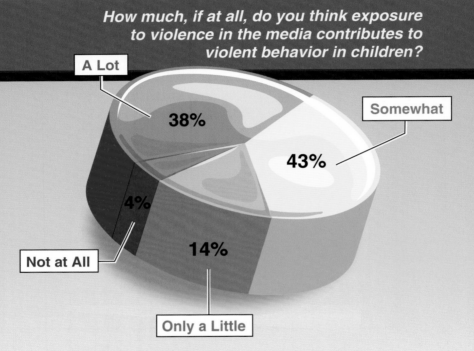

A Lot — 38%

Somewhat — 43%

4%

Not at All

14%

Only a Little

Source: Victoria Rideout, "Parents, Children & Media: A Kaiser Family Foundation Survey," *Kaiser Family Foundation*, June 2007. www.kff.org.

- The American Psychiatric Association finds that by age 18, an American youth will have seen **16,000 simulated murders** and 200,000 acts of violence in the media.

- Statistics from the U.S. Department of Justice show that the **violent crime rate** has been declining for the past 15 years.

- According to the Department of Justice, in 2005 U.S. residents aged 12 or older experienced approximately **5.2 million violent crimes**.

Exposure to Media Violence Increases Student Involvement in Physical Fighting

This chart is based on the results of a study of the effects of media violence on students. Students were surveyed twice within a time period of approximately six months. Based on the results of the surveys, researchers constructed this table to predict how exposure to sex and media violence increases the likelihood that students will be involved in physical fights.

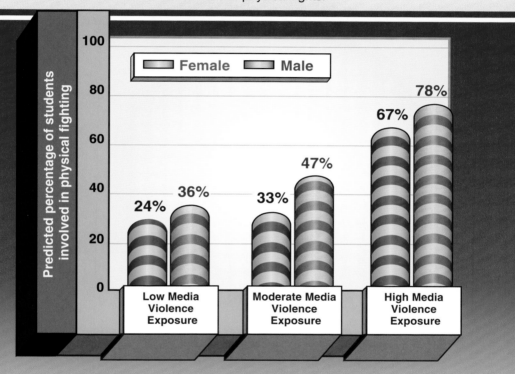

Source: Douglas A. Gentile et al., "Media Violence as a Risk Factor for Children: A Longitudinal Study," paper presented at the American Psychological Society 16th Annual Convention, Chicago, Illinois, May 2004.

- A 2007 Kaiser Family Foundation study shows that **43 percent of parents** think violent content contributes a lot to violent behavior in children.

- The American Psychological Association reports that cartoons average more than **80 violent acts per hour.**

Viewing Television Violence Increases the Likelihood of Violent Behavior

According to the results of this study by the University of Michigan Institute for Social Research, both women and men who were heavy childhood viewers of violent television shows are much more likely to have engaged in violent behavior at least once during the past year.

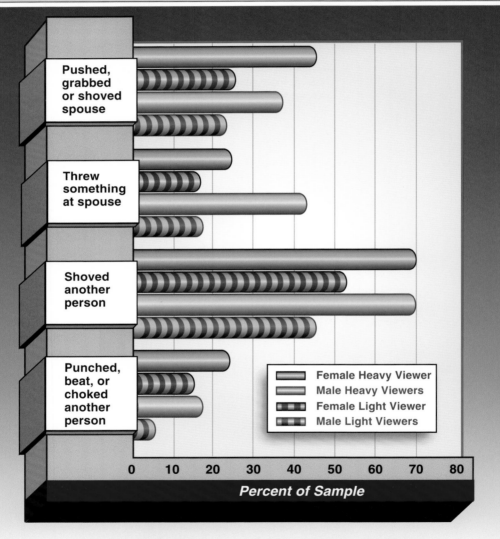

Pushed, grabbed or shoved spouse

Threw something at spouse

Shoved another person

Punched, beat, or choked another person

Female Heavy Viewer
Male Heavy Viewers
Female Light Viewer
Male Light Viewers

0   10   20   30   40   50   60   70   80

Percent of Sample

Source: Institute for Social Research, "The Long-Term Legacy of TV Violence," *ISR Research Update*, September 2006. www.isr.umich.edu.

Do Violent Video Games Inspire Violence?

Do Violent Video Games Inspire Violence?

❝It is more likely that aggressive people are *attracted* to violent media. Blaming violent media would be like going to the opera, noticing that most people there are rich, and concluding that opera makes people rich.❞

—Duke Ferris, "Caution: Children at Play: The Truth About Violent Youth and Video Games," *Game Revolution*, October 19, 2005. www.gamerevolution.com.

❝Dozens of experimental and correlational studies now document that violent video game play is related to increases in aggressive thoughts, feelings, and behaviors.❞

—National Institute on Media and the Family, "11th Annual MediaWise Video Game Report Card," November 28, 2006. www.mediafamily.org.

In 1998 the video game *Grand Theft Auto* (*GTA*) was released in the United States. The game allows the player to take on the role of a criminal who must commit various crimes, such as bank robberies and assassinations, and earn points for violent acts, such as killing a policeman. *GTA* and subsequent games in the series generated substantial controversy because of their violent content. As video game manufacturers release these and other violent games, debate continues over their effect on players. Critics disagree over whether research proves a link between violent games and violent behavior, the effects of active participation and new game technology, whether other factors are the real cause of violence, the benefits of video games, and the distinction between adult- and child-appropriate games.

Evidence for a Link Between Games and Violence

A number of researchers argue that their studies provide evidence of a link between violent video games and violent behavior. For example, in 2005 Jessica Nicoll and Kevin M. Kieffer of Saint Leo University in Florida found that when youth played violent video games, they showed more aggressive behavior after playing the games and tended to imitate the moves of the games. In a 2006 study at the Indiana University School of Medicine, researchers did brain scans of children who played a violent video game and found that for 30 minutes afterward the children exhibited an increase in emotional arousal and a decrease of activity in the parts of the brain that involve self-control, inhibition, and attention. Says psychologist Craig Anderson,

> " A number of researchers argue that their studies provide evidence of a link between violent video games and violent behavior. "

> There are all kinds of research teams around the world now who have found harmful effects, and unless one takes a very inaccurate view of the way scientists operate, one really can't dismiss all these research teams, many of which are headed up by top researchers in the field. The only people who really deny that there are these video-game violence effects, are people who don't have any real claim to expertise in the research area. The industry has to work very hard to find people that they then call experts, to contradict what the real experts say. . . . When you ask people who are identified as experts by those groups, they all come to the same conclusion: Yes, there are these harmful effects.[38]

Argument That No Link Exists Between Games and Violence

Some people insist that the evidence actually shows that video games do not cause violence. Seth Killian, a former national champion at the video game *Street Fighter*, believes that studies showing a link between violent games and violent behavior often use samples that are too small and make comparisons between very different games. In his opinion, real world experience shows that video games do not cause violence. For example, he says, there is no violence at video game tournaments. "Players scream, curse, and even hit the machines in disgust, but not each other."[39] In the opinion of Duke Ferris, who works in the video game industry, many people who criticize video game violence are simply afraid and misunderstand the games:

> Some people insist that . . . real world experience shows that video games do not cause violence.

Gaming is . . . a new medium, one that has recently become wildly successful. Young people play them and old folks don't understand, so they must be bad. Don't forget that in the 1950s, rock and roll was linked to youth violence in the same way. The hedonistic, tribal rhythms were going to turn America's youth into a bunch of violent maniacs. Rock and roll was banned and censored all over the country. A bill was even put before Congress in 1955 to ban rock and roll altogether.[40]

The Effect of Active Participation

Some people argue that video game violence has a greater impact than violence in other forms of media such as television or music, because video game players actively participate in the violence. As Anderson points out, "One of the real interesting differences between video games and film or television is that video games are necessarily interactive—they involve active participation by the game player." He explains, "The game player has to assume the identity of one of the violent characters and essentially has to make decisions and take physical action, whether it be squeezing the trigger on a toy gun, or clicking a mouse button." He says, "You are practicing all the aspects of violence: decision-making and carrying it out. . . . Practicing making a particular kind of decision, makes you better at making that kind of decision, just like practicing your multiplication tables makes you better at multiplication."[41] Psychiatrist Adolph Casal agrees, stating, "[Video game players] are not just releasing aggression. They are practicing aggression. When we practice something, we get good at it."[42]

Other Factors

Critics argue that because of the presence of many other influencing factors it is impossible to say violent video games cause violent behavior. In Ferris's opinion, even if research shows a correlation between aggression and violent media, it is impossible to say that the media actually caused the aggression. "Blaming violent media would be like going to the opera, noticing that most people there are rich, and concluding that opera makes people rich,"[43] he says. Many people believe that the reason a correlation is often observed between violent games and violent behavior is that violent people are often attracted to playing video games. According to a 2006 court decision, "It is impossible to determine from the data presented whether violent video games cause violence, or whether violent individuals are attracted to violent video games."[44] In the opinion of writer Neil Gerstein, some people simply have the tendency to commit violent acts, and whether they played violent video games has nothing to do with it. He says, "If a person is going to commit a violent act, then that person already had the propensity to commit violence all along."[45] In the opinion of Henry Jenkins, professor at the Massachusetts Institute of Technology, violent video games might contribute to violence, but there are many other factors involved: "I don't think video games in themselves are causing violence. It's another risk factor to contribute to the culture of violence."[46]

> " **Many people believe that . . . violent people are often attracted to playing video games.** "

The Effect of New Technology

Another concern is that as technology improves and video games have better graphics and become more realistic, violent content is having more of an impact on players. In the opinion of game developer Jonathan Harbour, "Playing a realistic game is similar to a real-world situation. That the U.S. Army is using first person shooters for recruitment and training is a telling point."[47] Others contend that while this theory may seem logical, in reality the opposite is true. Jenkins notes that paradoxically, the more realistic video games become, the less real the violence seems to the player. Jenkins says this is because the closer video game designers get to trying to reproduce the real world, the more critical players get about their failure to recreate the real. He also adds that because video games require that players use a game control, players are constantly reminded that they are merely playing a game and not interacting with the real world.

> "Another concern is that as . . . video games have better graphics and become more realistic, violent content is having more of an impact on players."

Possible Benefits of Video Games

Some people believe that rather than focusing on the possible harms of video games, society should recognize their benefits. They point out that video games can be both educational and therapeutic. In a 2004 study of the effects of video game violence reported in the *Journal of Young Investigators*, researcher Mickey Suhn Lee found that, "many gamers find playing video games a way to improve and practice their mental focus and attention. The increased stimulation also provides gamers with a way of actively mediating relaxation from diversion of stresses and focusing on a fun game."[48]

Adam Thierer, director of the Center for Digital Media Freedom, agrees that video games can be beneficial. He maintains, "From the Bible to Beowulf to Batman, depictions of violence have been used not only to teach lessons, but also to allow people—including children—to engage in a sort of escapism that can have a therapeutic effect on the human psyche."[49] Killian reports that in his experience as a game player, video games often help diffuse frustrations and give players a feeling of control of at least one aspect of their lives.

Games for Children Versus Games for Adults

In the video game controversy, some people take the position that yes, some violent video games might cause violent behavior in children, but that is because they are intended for adults only. While many children do play adult-only games, critics such as Pancho Eekels, creative director at video game company Digital Extremes, point out that the video game rating system designates some violent games for adults only because of the fact that they may be harmful for children. He critiques those parents who complain about these violent games, insisting that they are intended for adults only. Journalist Daphne White believes the problem is that although these games are rated for adults, they continue to be marketed to children. She argues, "Americans have decided not to market cigarettes, alcohol or pornography to minors. It's time we took the same public health position regarding children and media violence. Ultra-violent video games and movies should be marketed to adults only."[50]

> **Video games can be both educational and therapeutic.**

In Anderson's opinion, "A well-designed video game is an excellent teaching tool for a whole host of reasons. . . . But an excellent teaching tool teaches whatever the content is, whether for the benefit of society, or anti-social. And for the most part, violent video games are not the kinds of lessons we want America's children and adolescents to be learning."[51] Exactly what kind of lessons violent video games teach and whether they are desirable remains the topic of heated debate. Critics continue to debate the effects of video game violence, including whether research proves a link between violent games and violent behavior, the effects of active participation and new game technology, whether other factors are the real cause of violence, the benefits of video games, and the distinction between adult and child-appropriate games.

Primary Source Quotes*

Do Violent Video Games Inspire Violence?

> **So far, no one has been able to prove a direct link between video game violence and real-life violence . . . yet child-on-child violence has skyrocketed since the first video game was released.**

—Christine, "Do Video Games Inspire Violence?" *Chris Vs Chris: A Battle of the Minds and Sexes*, January 1, 2006. www.chrisvschris.com.

Christine is a television writer and also writes for the Web site *Chris Vs Chris: A Battle of the Minds and Sexes.*

> **Violent crime is at the lowest it has been in a good thirty years. . . . In other words, the PlayStation era has, in fact, produced the most *non-violent* kids ever.**

—Duke Ferris, "Caution: Children at Play: The Truth About Violent Youth and Video Games," *Game Revolution*, October 19, 2005. www.gamerevolution.com.

Ferris works in the video game industry.

Bracketed quotes indicate conflicting positions.

* Editor's Note: While the definition of a primary source can be narrowly or broadly defined, for the purposes of Compact Research, a primary source consists of: 1) results of original research presented by an organization or researcher; 2) eyewitness accounts of events, personal experience, or work experience; 3) first-person editorials offering pundits' opinions; 4) government officials presenting political plans and/or policies; 5) representatives of organizations presenting testimony or policy.

66**There is no showing whatsoever that video games, in the absence of other violent media, cause even the slightest injury to children.**99

—James M. Rosenbaum, opinion, U.S. District Court for the District of Minnesota, *ESA et al. v. Hatch et al.,* July 2006.

Rosenbaum is a chief district judge for the District of Minnesota.

66**It is very likely that children, after playing . . . [violent video] games . . . remain restless and as a result show aggressive behavior in their play and interaction with other children.**99

—Patti M. Valkenburg, *Children's Responses to the Screen: A Media Psychological Approach.* Mahwah, NJ: Lawrence Erlbaum, 2004, p. 134.

Valkenburg is a professor at the Amsterdam School of Communications Research.

66**The increased stimulation [of playing video games] . . . provides gamers with a way of actively mediating relaxation from diversion of stresses and focusing on a fun game.**99

—Mickey Suhn Lee, "Effects of Video Game Violence on Prosocial and Antisocial Behaviors," *Journal of Young Investigators*, August 2004.

Lee is a researcher for the *Journal of Young Investigators*, a journal that publishes research by undergraduate students.

66I'm a life-long video game player and . . . I've seen
the effects of violent video games, and on a scale far
broader than any laboratory experiment. . . . The tournaments [have] . . . zero physically violent incidents.
. . . There's no evidence that these players are more
violent in other settings than any other cross-section
of the population, either.99

—Seth Killian, "Violent Video Game Players Mysteriously Avoid Killing Selves, Others," *NCAC Censorship News*, Winter
2003/2004. www.ncac.org.

Killian is a video game player and former national champion at the video game
Street Fighter.

66[With] violent video games . . . you are practicing all
the aspects of violence: decision-making and carrying
it out. . . . Practicing making a particular kind of decision, makes you better at making that kind of decision, just like practicing your multiplication tables
makes you better at multiplication.99

—Craig Anderson, "The Research Is In: Violent Video Games Can Lead to Violent Behavior," *Executive Intelligence
Review*, June 1, 2007. www.larouchepub.com.

Anderson is a professor of psychology at Iowa State University and author of
*Violent Video Game Effects on Children and Adolescents: Theory, Research, and
Public Policy*.

66As long as children develop moral values and are giv-
en guidance and love by their parents or parent, then
all of the violent video games in the world would not
have a negative effect on them.99

—Neil Gerstein, "Do Video Games Lead to Violence or Not?" *EzineArticles.com*, May 25, 2007. http://ezinearticles.com.

Gerstein is a contributing writer for *EzineArticles.com*, a Web site that offers a
collection of articles on various topics.

"The results of the study . . . [show that] students who play more violent video games are more likely to have been involved in physical fights and get into arguments with teachers more frequently."

—Douglas A. Gentile et al., "The Effects of Video Game Habits on Adolescent Hostility, Aggressive Behaviors, and School Performance," *Journal of Adolescence*, vol. 27, 2004, p. 18.

Gentile is director of research at the National Institute on Media and the Family.

"Spending large amounts of time playing . . . [video] games can create problems and lead to . . . aggressive thoughts and behaviors."

—American Academy of Child & Adolescent Psychiatry, "Children and Video Games: Playing with Violence," August 2006. www.aacap.org.

The American Academy of Child & Adolescent Psychiatry is a national medical association dedicated to treating and improving the quality of life for children with mental, behavioral, or developmental disorders.

"[It is likely that] violence causes the games instead of it being the other way around. What came first? Car jacking or *Grand Theft Auto*? It's not really a stretch to comprehend the fact that the games we see today are a product of our society and not the other way around."

—William, "Violence Causes Games," *Gaming Today*, June 11, 2007. http ://news.filefront.com.

William is a contributor to *Gaming Today*, a Web site that posts news and information related to video games.

> **"Recent studies show that violent games only increase your kids' aggression if they already have pre-existing behavioral problems."**

—Clive Thomson, "You Grew Up Playing Shoot'em-Up Games. Why Can't Your Kids?" *Wired*, April 9, 2007. www.wired.com.

Thomson is a contributing writer for *New York Times Magazine* and a regular contributor to *Wired* and *New York* magazines.

> **"As human beings (not as gamers) there is a distinct realization between video game violence and real life violence. People in general do not want to bring harm to one another for no reason and playing a video game simply isn't a large enough reason to force someone out of the comfort of their living room and onto a sidewalk with a shotgun."**

—Rashawn Blanchard, "Video Games and Violence: Not Causing Tragedies Since 1971," *Associated Content*, May 1, 2007. www.associatedcontent.com.

Blanchard is a contributing writer for the Web site *Associated Content*.

> **"I'm 15 and if I even *think* of getting into an angry mood or something else, it's always the games that caused it. . . . Games are the scapegoat for everyone."**

—TheCritic9392, "Why We Don't Need the ESRB," *GameSpot*, June 20, 2007. www.gamespot.com.

TheCritic9392 is the online identity of an anonymous 15-year-old video game player.

Facts and Illustrations

Do Violent Video Games Inspire Violence?

- According to the Entertainment Software Association in 2006, **93 percent of computer game buyers** and 83 percent of console game buyers are over the age of 18.

- Nielsen Media Research reports that of those people with a television in their home, **70 percent** of 2- to 11-year-olds and almost **80 percent** of 12- to 17-year-olds have a video game console.

- The National Institute on Media and the Family finds that **7 out of 10** children report playing M-rated games.

- Sales of video games have more than doubled since 1996, rising to **$7.3 billion** in 2004.

- In a 2005 review of the existing research on the effects of violent video games, Douglas Gentile finds that many of the studies have a sample of fewer than **200 participants**, increasing the chance of misleading results.

- In a 2004 meta-analysis of video game research Craig Anderson found that **violent video game playing** and aggression are significantly related.

- In a 2006 study of the effects of video game violence on **100 students ages 18 to 20**, Sonya Brady found that playing a violent game did not affect attitudes toward violence.

Youth Video Game Playing Is Substantial

Data from a Kaiser Family Foundation survey reveal that more than 50 percent of youth ages 8 to 18 play video or computer games, and that the average playing time is approximately 1 hour per day. Eight-to-10-year-olds have the highest playing time per day.

	Average Time/Day	Proportion playing any video or computer game	Proportion playing 1+ hours/day
Age			
8-to-10-year-olds	1:25	65%	34%
11-to-14-year-olds	1:09	63%	31%
15-to-18-year-olds	0:52	49%	24%
Gender			
Boys	1:34	68%	41%
Girls	0:40	51%	18%
Race			
White	1:03	61%	28%
Black	1:26	60%	37%
Hispanic	1:10	55%	29%
Parent Education			
High school or less	1:09	59%	30%
Some college	0:50	52%	24%
College graduate	1:16	63%	31%
Income			
Under $35,000	0:59	59%	31%
$35,000–$50,000	1:09	56%	28%
Over $50,000	1:13	65%	30%
Total	**1:08**	**59%**	**30%**

Source: Donald F. Roberts, Ulla G. Foehr, and Victoria Rideout, "Generation M: Media in the Lives of 8–18-Year-Olds," *Kaiser Family Foundation*, March 2005. www.kff.org.

Much of Youth Video Game Playing Is Unsupervised

According to this survey conducted by the Institute on Media and the Family, while more than 50 percent of parents report that they supervise children's video game playing, a significant number of children report that they play video games unsupervised.

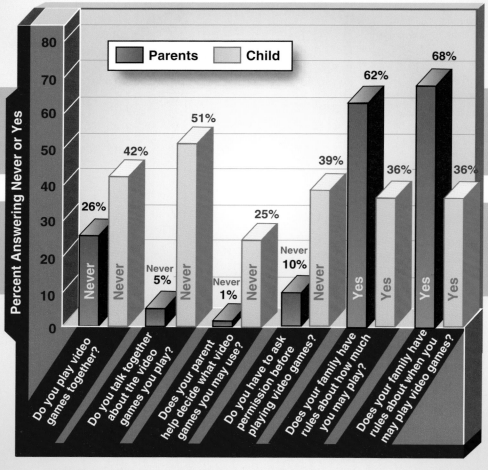

Parents   Child

Percent Answering Never or Yes

- 26% Never — Do you play video games together?
- 42% Never — Do you talk together about the video games you play?
- 5% Never
- 51% Never — Does your parent help decide what video games you may use?
- 1% Never
- 25% Never — Do you have to ask permission before playing video games?
- 10% Never
- 39% Yes — Does your family have rules about how much you may play?
- 62% Yes
- 36% Yes
- 68% Yes — Does your family have rules about when you may play video games?
- 36% Yes

Source: David Walsh et al. "11th Annual MediaWise Video Game Report Card," *Institute on Media and the Family*, November 28, 2006. www.mediafamily.org.

Violent Crime Is Decreasing as Video Game Violence Increases

This graph compares the violent crime rate in the United States with the availability of video game devices Playstation 1 and Playstation 2, and the violent video games *Grand Theft Auto 1* and *Grand Theft Auto 3*. It reveals that at the same time as these game devices and violent games have become available, the crime rate has decreased.

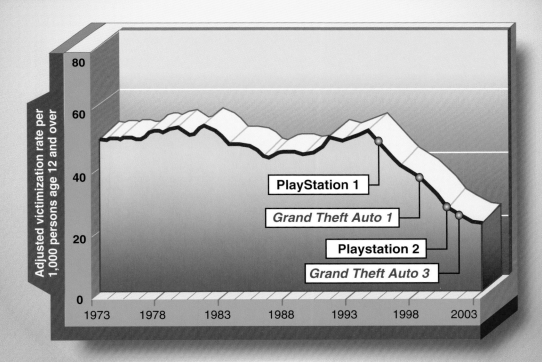

Source: Duke Ferris, "Caution: Children at Play: The Truth About Youth and Video Games," *Game Revolution*, October 19, 2005. www.gamerevolution.com.

• According to the National Institute on Media and the Family, playing a large amount of violent video games increases children's risk of physical aggression in school by **42 percent** compared to those who do not play violent games.

Violent Video Games Increase Aggression

This graph shows the results of an analysis of numerous studies on the effects of video games on aggressive behavior and other aggression-related variables. It shows that on average, playing violent video games increases aggressive behavior, hostile affect, physiological arousal, and aggressive thoughts.

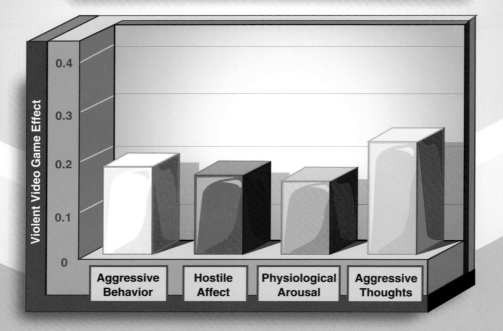

Source: Craig Anderson, "Violence in the Media: Its Effects on Children," *Victoria Parenting Centre and Young Media Australia*, 2004. www.parentingrc.org.au.

- According to a 2004 study published in the *Journal of Adolescence*, researchers found that of those students with a high level of hostility, **63 percent** of those exposed to a large amount of video game violence had been involved in physical fights, while only **28 percent** of those with low video game exposure had been.

- The National Center for Education Statistics reports that between 1993 and 2003 the percentage of students who reported being in a fight anywhere declined—from **42 percent** in 1993 to **33 percent** in 2003.

Is Current Regulation of Media Violence Effective?

> ❝It is a little frustrating when we have this data that demonstrates there is a clear public health connection between exposure to violence and increased aggression that we have been as a society unable to come up with any adequate public health response.❞

—Hillary Rodham Clinton, "Senator Clinton's Speech to Kaiser Family Foundation upon Release of *Generation M: Media in the Lives of Kids 8 to 18*," March 8, 2005.

> ❝[Regulation of media violence] would . . . [have] a significant chilling effect on broadcasters' programming and editorial decisions, with less creative and informative programming for the American public.❞

—David H. Solomon, "No Violence to the First Amendment," *Broadcasting & Cable*, June 18, 2007.

In the United States the government does not restrict violent content in the media. Instead, existing regulation occurs through voluntary industry-established systems such as the Entertainment Software Rating Board, which rates video games, or the Motion Picture Association of America, which rates movies. It also occurs when parents restrict their children's media access. However the current system is the subject of much controversy. Disagreement is widespread over whether the various industry rating systems are a good way for society to deal with the issue of media violence, and the effectiveness of parental monitoring is intensely debated.

Public Opinion

Surveys of public opinion show that many Americans believe violent content in the media is excessive. For example, according to a 2005 *Time* magazine poll, 66 percent of Americans believed there is too much violence on television. Much of the concern is related to children's exposure to this violent content. A 2005 survey conducted by the Pew Research Center found that more than half of the respondents were concerned about the content—including violence—that children are exposed to in the media. They were particularly concerned over Internet content, and two-thirds of those surveyed believed the content of television shows had gotten worse than it was five years before.

> " **Disagreement is widespread over whether the various industry rating systems are a good way for society to deal with the issue of media violence.** "

Movie Ratings

The Motion Picture Association of America (MPAA), which is responsible for rating movies in the United States, maintains that its rating system effectively identifies violent content in movies so that parents and others can make informed decisions about the movies they watch. The ratings board is comprised of an anonymous group of parents. Joan Graves, chairman of the MPAA's Classification and Ratings Administration, describes these anonymous members: "The ideal person is out in the community getting feedback from other parents. . . . We're looking for parents with solid judgment who want to raise healthy kids and know that a lot goes into it."[52] In response to critiques that movie violence has increased while ratings have stayed the same, the MPAA says,

> The rating system is a flexible one, meant to consider parental attitudes at the time the motion picture is rated. . . .

Thus, you may notice, for example, that as the concerns of parents about teen drug use or sexual activity increase, motion pictures which contain elements of illicit drug abuse or strong sexual content will be assigned a higher rating, reflecting the views of American parents.[53]

Critics contend that movie ratings are not always accurate and consistent and that movie watchers cannot depend on them when deciding whether to view a movie. For example, in a 2005 study researchers at the School of Public Health at the University of California at Los Angeles concluded that movie ratings did not provide much meaningful guidance on violent content. They found significant violent content in a number of movies rated appropriate for children. In the opinion of researcher Theresa Webb, "The movie industry's rating system and its prose explanations frequently hide more offensive elements behind euphemistic and innocuous terminology."[54]

Television Ratings

Like movie ratings, television ratings also have numerous defenders and critics. Some people insist that the ratings are comprehensive and easy to use. In addition to being encrypted in television programming, television ratings are displayed on the screen at the beginning of programs and included in electronic program guides. According to Kyle McSlarrow, president of the National Cable & Telecommunications Association, "With ratings and program guides, program networks and operators make it easy to identify programming that may, in one respect or another, be deemed unsuitable for children."[55] He also points out that in June 2005, ratings were improved by increasing the size of the ratings icon on the television screen and by inserting the icon on the screen after every commercial break. Further, says McSlarrow, the cable industry has launched a num-

> " Critics contend that movie ratings are not always accurate and consistent and that movie watchers cannot depend on them when deciding whether to view a movie. "

ber of initiatives to help educate parents about using ratings.

Yet many people contend that ratings are inconsistent and incomplete. In the opinion of Federal Communications Commission (FCC) commissioner Deborah Taylor Tate, because ratings are not administered by a standardized board, they are often ineffective: "Individual networks rate each of their programs, leading to inconsistencies across channels, and even across shows. . . . For example, a program may very well have violent content, but if the network does not believe it constitutes 'moderate' violence, a 'V' label is not applied."[56]

Video Game Ratings

There are numerous critics of the video game rating system. The primary critique is that while violent video games are often rated for adults or older youth only, younger children commonly play them. For example, the National Institute on Media and the Family found that 87 percent of teenage and preteen boys play games rated "M," which are recommended for those over age 17. Senator Hillary Rodham Clinton believes that the ratings system needs more power, so that instead of merely recommending who should play a particular game, it actually stops children from acquiring and playing inappropriate games. She says, "The video game industry has already decided that games rated M and AO are not appropriate for young people. That's what the labels M and AO mean. I am emphasizing that ratings should have meaning and they should be enforced. A 7 year old should not be able to walk into Wal-mart and buy [violent game] *Grand Theft Auto*."[57]

> "Some people insist that the [television] ratings are comprehensive and easy to use.

The video game industry and its defenders contend that the rating system works. In the opinion of Adam Thierer, director of the Center for Digital Media Freedom, video game ratings are detailed and prominently displayed, making evaluation of the game easy. He says, "A quick glance at the back of any game box provides parents with plenty of information to make decisions for their families."[58] In response to the critique that many children are able to access inappropriate violent games, the Entertainment Software Association (ESA), which established the video game rating board, contends that if children are playing violent games rated for adults, it is the fault of the parents, not the rating system. According to the ESA, the average video game buyer is 40 years old. In addition, it says, parents are involved in the purchase or rental of games 83 percent of the time, and 90 percent of games are purchased by people over age 18. "In other words, in an overwhelming majority of instances, parents are ultimately making the decisions about what games their kids acquire."[59]

> ❝ **[Critics charge that] while violent video games are often rated for adults or older youth only, younger children commonly play them.** ❞

Internet

Violence on the Internet is an issue of increasing concern for society. Many people are worried that because the Internet is largely unregulated, any user can easily access the large variety of violent content it offers. Filters are the primary method of blocking violent media content. Software filters exist that allow users to block violent content, restrict their children's e-mail, limit the amount of time spent on the Internet, and track the Internet sites visited. However, these filters often block educational and harmless content as well, prompting numerous critics to oppose their use. According to the congressionally appointed COPA Commission, which was established to identify ways to limit children's access to harmful material on the Internet,

> Filters are not a particularly effective technology for protecting children from objectionable Internet content. Further, such programs also block a substantial percentage of web pages with no objectionable material. Overall, filters failed to block objectionable content 25 percent of the time, while on the other hand, they improperly blocked 21 percent of benign content.[60]

Violent music lyrics are identified by a voluntary album label that states, "Parental Advisory: Explicit Content." However, people disagree over the effectiveness of this label. Critics point out that there is no law restricting the sale of music with the sticker. While some shops refuse to sell these albums to children, many do not. The Recording Industry Association of America (RIAA), which supplies the labels, contends that enforcement is the domain of parents. It insists that the Parental Advisory label provides parents with adequate information about music content and that the rest is the parents' responsibility. RIAA CEO Mitch Bainwol says,

> All music is not always appropriate for all ages. The music industry takes seriously its responsibility to help parents determine what is and is not appropriate for their children. That's why the record companies created the Parental Advisory Label Program. This program is a tool to help parents make the choice about when—and whether—their children should be able to listen to a particular recording.[61]

Parental Monitoring

Some people believe that parental monitoring of children's media consumption is effectively regulating media violence. Numerous statistics show that many parents do monitor their children's media use. For example, according to a 2006 Pew Internet & American Life Project survey of teenage media use, 77 percent of parents have rules about what television shows their children can watch, 67 percent about the type of video games played, and 85 percent about the Web sites they can visit. Thierer concludes that, "almost all parents enforce a variety of household media rules and have guidelines for acceptable media consumption."[62] According to David Bickham, research scientist at the Center on Media and Child Health at Harvard Medical School, such monitoring works. He says that a large body of research shows that when parents actively monitor and participate in their

> " **Because the Internet is largely unregulated, any user can easily access the large variety of violent content it offers.** "

children's media use, the harmful effects of violence are reduced.

Critics contend that in reality the majority of parents are not monitoring their children's media use. According to a 2004 study published in *Pediatrics*, researchers surveyed 1,004 adults and found that the majority of parents said their children see fighting, guns, and other violence on television. Fewer than half of the surveyed parents reported watching television with their children. A March 2005 study by the Kaiser Family Foundation shows that despite the fact that many parents express concerns about their children's media usage, the children do not report much parental monitoring of their media consumption. After looking at the study results, the organization concludes that either parents are not truly concerned about their children's media usage, or they have simply given up trying to regulate it, but either way there is not much regulation going on.

"Numerous statistics show that many parents do monitor their children's media use."

Industry Self-Regulation

Some people believe that the various media industries effectively regulate violent content. Thierer points out that while people critique the media industry, charging that it should do more to address concerns about media violence, it is already doing quite a lot through parental controls such as the V-chip, personal video recorders, and rating systems. He also believes that this effort is superior to what the government could do. "Not only are markets bringing parents empowering tools to restrict or tailor media content in their homes," he says, "but this is being done much more quickly, much more closely tailored to the parents' own desires, and without concerns about censorship such as is associated with traditional government regulatory efforts."[63] Peter Suderman, managing editor of *National Review Online*, insists that the media industry has effectively regulated violent content in the past and will continue to do so. He says, "Industry ratings boards like the ESRB and the MPAA ought to be free to self-police without bureaucratic meddling. And in fact, this is just what they've done."[64]

Others believe that self-regulation of violent content by the media is not working. In the opinion of Senator Hillary Rodham Clinton, because the media is motivated by profit, it will continue to produce increasingly violent content:

> We know that left to their own devices, you have to keep upping the ante on violence because people do get desensitized and children are going to want more and more stimulation. And unfortunately in a free market like ours, what sells will become even more violent, and the companies will ratchet up the violence in order to increase ratings and sales figures.[65]

While society continues to express concern over the availability of violent media content, people disagree over the effectiveness of the current regulatory system. Each industry-established rating system is the subject of both praise and criticism, and significant disagreement exists over the effectiveness of parental monitoring of children's media consumption.

Is Current Regulation of Media Violence Effective?

"Nationwide scientific polls, conducted each year . . . have consistently given the [movie] rating program high marks by parents throughout the land. . . . The ratings board will continue to strive to rate movies in a way that they as parents would approve of when making choices about films suitable for their families."

—Motion Picture Association of America, "How Movies Are Rated," 2005. www.mppa.org.

The Motion Picture Association of America is a trade association that represents the six major movie studios in the United States.

"Based on my research, I believe that the existing [movie] ratings systems provide useful information for parents, but I also see large opportunities for improvement."

—Kim Thomson, "Effectiveness of Media Rating Systems," congressional testimony, September 28, 2004.

Thomson is an associate professor and director of the Kids Risk Project at the Harvard School of Public Health.

Bracketed quotes indicate conflicting positions.

* Editor's Note: While the definition of a primary source can be narrowly or broadly defined, for the purposes of Compact Research, a primary source consists of: 1) results of original research presented by an organization or researcher; 2) eyewitness accounts of events, personal experience, or work experience; 3) first-person editorials offering pundits' opinions; 4) government officials presenting political plans and/or policies; 5) representatives of organizations presenting testimony or policy.

66Before I was a parent myself, I paid little attention to the MPAA Ratings. As a parent, I quickly became horrified as how unusable the ratings were in helping to decide what films I could and could not take my daughter to.99

—Robert Moore, "They See No Evil," Amazon.com customer review, May 3, 2007. www.amazon.com.

Moore is a book reviewer who lives in Chicago.

66[In] the cable industry . . . we take seriously our responsibility to ensure that parents have the tools they need to decide what is suitable for their families and to prevent their children from watching programming they deem unsuitable.99

—Kyle McSlarrow, "Images Children See on the Screen," testimony before the U.S. House of Representatives Subcommittee on Telecommunications and the Internet, Washington D.C., June 22, 2007.

McSlarrow is president of the National Cable & Telecommunications Association.

66[The television ratings system has] proven to be insufficient to protect our children. . . . The industry should implement ratings reliably, more completely, consistently, and accurately.99

—Deborah Taylor Tate, statement regarding "Violent Television Programming and Its Impact on Children," Federal Communications Commission, April 6, 2007. www.fcc.gov.

Tate is a commissioner for the Federal Communications Commission, a government agency with the primary goal of protecting American consumers.

"Video game ratings and restrictions are pretty much a joke. . . . I've never ever had an online game merchant, store, vendor or seller ask me how old I was prior to buying a video game. . . . And . . . have you ever been asked to show identification when renting a video game? I haven't. My kids haven't. . . . The standards are there but no one really pays attention to them."

—*Epinions.com*, "Video Game Violence, Bare Breasted Women & Thermonuclear War," November 24, 2004. www.epinions.com.

This opinion was posted at *Epinions.com* by an unnamed contributor.

"We remain extremely proud of the ESRB rating system and the information it provides. . . . Millions of parents rely on ESRB ratings to choose games they deem appropriate for their children and families, and we value greatly the trust they have placed in our ratings."

—Patricia E. Vance, "Violent and Explicit Video Games: Informing Parents and Protecting Children," testimony before the U.S. House of Representatives Subcommittee on Commerce, Trade and Consumer Protection, June 14, 2006.

Vance is president of the Entertainment Software Rating Board, which rates video games in the United States.

"Unlike the motion picture industry, the video game industry has not developed an effective self-regulation system that keeps adult material out of the hands of children."

—Out-Law.com, "Video Games and Age Restrictions—the US and UK," September 2006. www.out-law.com.

Out-Law.com is a Web site maintained by international law firm Pinsent Masons.

66The . . . [current video game rating] system lets the people who know their content the best—the publishers—take responsibility for disclosing what is in the product. There is no better way to do this.99

—Warren W. Buckleitner, "Violent and Explicit Video Games: Informing Parents and Protecting Children," congressional testimony, June 14, 2006.

Buckleitner is a software reviewer and editor of *Children's Technology Review*.

66Media violence is a public health issue that affects all our children. . . . [Parents need to] take action to reduce media violence in children's lives.99

—Teachers Resisting Unhealthy Children's Entertainment, "Media Violence and Children Action Guide, 2004–2005." www.truceteachers.org.

Teachers Resisting Unhealthy Children's Entertainment is an organization of early childhood professionals that works to promote a positive play environment for children. It believes media violence has a negative impact on children.

66Most parents feel they are doing the best they can to keep a check on the role media are playing in their children's lives. . . . They feel like they're doing a pretty good job of protecting their own children.99

—Victoria Rideout, "Parents, Children & Media: A Kaiser Family Foundation Survey," Kaiser Family Foundation, June 2007. www.kff.org.

Rideout is vice president of the Kaiser Family Foundation, an organization that focuses on major health issues affecting the United States.

66[There is] widespread exposure of children and young teens to advertising that promotes albums and recordings with an explicit-content [such as violence] label. . . . Moreover, few retailers appear to have in place effective policies to prevent children from buying these products.99

—Federal Trade Commission, "Marketing Violent Entertainment to Children," April 2007. www.ftc.gov.

The Federal Trade Commission is a government agency with the primary goal of protecting American consumers.

66Kids are exposed to a continuum of violence on the Internet, ranging from sites with sophomoric cruel humour to disturbing depiction of torture and sadism. Today, children and teens can download violent music lyrics . . . and access violent images, video clips and online games, with the click of a mouse.99

—Be Web Aware, "Violent and Hateful Content," 2007. www.bewebaware.ca.

Be Web Aware is a national Canadian public education program on Internet safety.

Facts and Illustrations

Is Current Regulation of Media Violence Effective?

- The Kids Risk Project at the **Harvard Public School of Health** reports that between 1992 and 2003 a significant increase in violent content was found in movies rated "P" and "PG-13."

- According to the **Motion Picture Association of America, 78 percent** of parents with children under age 13 find the movie rating system "very useful" to "fairly useful" in helping them make decisions about what movies their children see.

- According to president of the National Cable & Telecommunications Association Kyle McSlarrow, since 2005 the cable industry has donated air time valued at more than **$300 million** in order in educate the public about parental controls, television ratings, and the V-chip.

- In a 2007 report on prime-time television ratings, the Parents Television Council finds that **42 percent** of shows containing violence lack the "V" descriptor.

- The Entertainment Software Rating Board reports that parents agree with video game ratings **82 percent** of the time, while another 5 percent of the time the ratings are thought to be too strict.

- A 2005 survey by the Media Awareness Network reveals that approximately **33 percent** of the favorite Internet sites listed by kids contain material that is violent.

Television Ratings Fail to Identify All Violent/Sexual Content

In these key findings from a 2007 review of the reliability and consistency of television ratings on prime-time broadcast television, the Parents Television Council reveals that many television shows have violent content that is not identified by the ratings system.

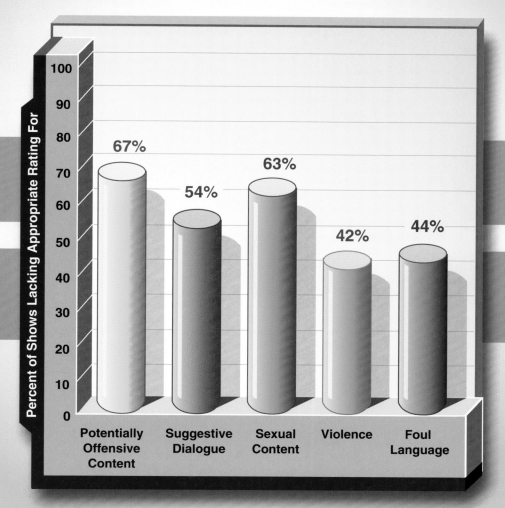

Source: Parents Television Council, "The Ratings Sham II," April 16, 2007. www.parentstv.org.

67

Majority of Video Games Are Appropriate for Youth

According to this graph provided by the Entertainment Software Rating Board, the majority of the video games released in 2005 are appropriate for children, and do not contain the intense violence that might appear in Mature (M) and Adults Only (AO) rated games. The graph shows that only 12 percent of the 2005 games are rated M, and less than 1 percent are rated AO.

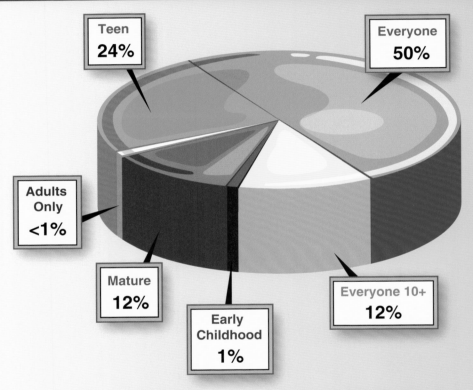

Teen
24%

Everyone
50%

Adults Only
<1%

Mature
12%

Early Childhood
1%

Everyone 10+
12%

Source: Patricia E. Vance, "Violent and Explicit Video Games: Informing Parents and Protecting Children," testimony before the U.S. House of Representatives, Subcommittee on Commerce, Trade and Consumer Protection, June 14, 2006. www.esrb.org.

- In a 2007 survey of 1,008 parents the Kaiser Family Foundation found that two-thirds of parents say they **"closely monitor"** their children's media use, and only 18 percent believe they should do more than they do now.

Most Music Videos Do Not Contain Violent Images

This chart presents the results of an analysis of the content of music videos from four popular Web sites. The researcher analyzed 952 music videos and found that while a significant percentage of music videos contain violent content, the majority (84 percent) of those analyzed had no violent content.

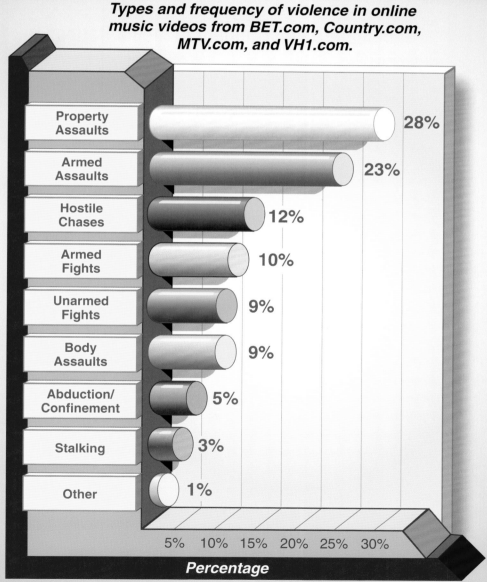

Types and frequency of violence in online music videos from BET.com, Country.com, MTV.com, and VH1.com.

- Property Assaults — 28%
- Armed Assaults — 23%
- Hostile Chases — 12%
- Armed Fights — 10%
- Unarmed Fights — 9%
- Body Assaults — 9%
- Abduction/Confinement — 5%
- Stalking — 3%
- Other — 1%

5% 10% 15% 20% 25% 30%

Percentage

Source: Debashis Aikat, "Streaming Violent Genres Online: Visual Images in Music Videos on BET.com, Country.com, MTV.com, and VH1.com," *Popular Music and Society*, vol. 27, no. 2, 2004.

- In a 2004 *Pediatrics* article researchers report that from a survey of **1,004 parents, 53 percent** report always limiting violent television viewing.

- In 2006 the **National Institute on Media and the Family** found that while most parents say they always help decide what video games their children may buy, only **30 percent** of children say their parents do.

Incomplete Enforcement of Media Ratings

Data from a Federal Trade Commission study reveals that ratings from movies, DVDs, music, and video games are not always posted or enforced. The study found that a significant number of children were able to purchase these products even though they were too young to qualify for the age rating.

Product		R-rated movies at the theater (Percent of 250 shoppers)	R-rated movies on DVD (Percent of 252 shoppers)	Unrated movies on DVD (Percent of 101 shoppers)	Music (Percent of 249 shoppers)	Games (Percent of 657 shoppers)
Question 1. Was rating information posted?	NO	44%	81%	79%	83%	59%
	YES	56%	19%	21%	17%	41%
Question 2. Was the child able to make a purchase?	NO	61%	29%	29%	24%	58%
	YES	39%	71%	71%	76%	42%
Question 2. Did an employee ask the child's age?	NO	44%	72%	72%	79%	49%
	YES	56%	28%	28%	21%	51%

Source: Federal Trade Commission, "Marketing Violent Entertainment to Children," April 2007. www.ftc.gov.

- According to the Parents Television Council, **44 percent** of kids say they watch something different when they are alone than with their parents.

- According to a 2006 study by the National Institute on Media and the Family, **92 percent** of stores say they have a policy preventing children under age 17 from renting or buying "M" rated video games.

- The Federal Trade Commission reports that in a 2004 study, **69 percent** of unaccompanied **13-to-16-year-olds** were able to purchase "M" rated video games from retailers.

How Can the Problems Associated with Media Violence Be Reduced?

❝ It is time—in fact, it is long past time—for . . . meaningful action on media violence.❞

—Michael J. Copps, remarks to the Parents Television Council, Washington, D.C., January 10, 2007.

❝ Decisions about acceptable media content are extraordinarily personal; no two people will have the same set of values. . . . The ultimate decision about acceptable content [should be left to the individual].❞

—Adam Thierer, "The Right Way to Regulate Violent TV," Progress & Freedom Foundation, May 2007. www.pff.org.

Despite the controversy it generates, violence in the media seems to be an integral part of life. As Federal Communications Commission (FCC) commissioner Robert M. McDowell points out, "We live in an often violent world. News reports, documentaries and other television programs must address violent topics, almost by necessity."[66] Since media violence does not appear to be going away, society takes various measures to reduce the problems associated with it. However, tremendous disagreement exists among researchers, policy makers, and the general public regarding exactly what measures should be taken. Many different opinions are given regarding the desirability and effectiveness of reducing the overall level of media violence; parental supervision of children's media use; government regulation and whether this is desirable, feasible, or even constitutional; V-chip and television ratings; and industry self-regulation.

Overall Level of Media Violence

Some people insist that the best way to reduce the problems associated with media violence is to reduce the overall amount of media violence. They argue that media content has become more and more violent in past years and that it is thus impossible for media consumers not to be subject to violent material. Others contend that not only is reducing media violence an ineffective solution, but it violates the freedom of consumers to choose their media content. In the opinion of director of the Center for Digital Media Freedom Adam Thierer, "Absent removing all media devices from a home, it would be impossible to eliminate all unwanted or unexpected encounters from life."[67] Instead, he argues, the choice about media content should be left up to the individual consumer, because everyone will make different decisions about what is acceptable. While many people argue that violence should be reduced to protect children, others point out that many media consumers are adults, not children. For example, the organization TV Watch finds that 68 percent of television-viewing households in the United States do not include any children under age 18. Critics argue that it would be unfair to restrict the media use of so many adults just to protect children.

> " Since media violence does not appear to be going away, society takes various measures to reduce the problems associated with it. "

Many people believe that media violence primarily harms children and that the best way to reduce this harm is for parents to supervise their children's media use. In a 2007 statement McDowell stresses the importance of parental supervision: "Parents should be the first and last line of defense in protecting their children from excessively violent content. . . . While government can and should do all that it can to protect children, parents should not shirk their primary responsibility to be actively engaged in their upbringing."[68] Thierer agrees, saying, "If Parents bring media devices into the home and then give their kids free rein, that's just poor parenting. . . . Parents don't bring other products home—such as cars, weapons, liquor, or various chemicals—and then expect the government to assume responsibility from there."[69]

> **While many people argue that violence should be reduced to protect children, others point out that many media consumers are adults, not children.**

Critics contend that parental supervision is not enough to prevent children's exposure to violent media. In the opinion of the *Christian Science Monitor*, "Yes, parents have an obligation to supervise their kids' viewing. . . . [But] to simply state that parents alone are responsible for controlling their kids' access to media violence is also to say they should be responsible for things such as safe streets."[70] FCC commissioner Jonathan S. Adelstein points out that even if parents are responsibly monitoring their children's media use, children are sometimes exposed to violent content. For example, he says, "I fully understand that it is my choice to turn the television on or off. . . . Sometimes, though, it is a trailer for a news show or a promotion for a horror movie that comes on during what was considered safe family programming."[71]

Government Regulation

Advocates of government regulation of media violence say that the industry is not regulating responsibly, so it is time for the government to step in. While the government does not currently regulate media violence, in a 2007 report the FCC finds that some regulation might be necessary and suggests that Congress might draft a definition of violence for regulatory purposes.

However, there are many opponents to government regulation. Marv

Johnson, a legislative counsel for the American Civil Liberties Union (ACLU) believes that the government will not be able to regulate effectively: "[The government has] had a poor record of being able to define indecency and enforce what is and isn't indecent. . . . Now they want to muck about in what is and isn't violence. . . . The government always tends to use a blunt instrument when it regulates something, rather than a scalpel."[72] In a 2007 press release Caroline Fredrickson, director of the ACLU Washington Legislative Office, argues that it is the responsibility of parents, not government, to regulate children's exposure to media violence: "Government should not parent the parents."[73]

Feasibility of Government Regulation

Even if the majority of society decided that it was desirable for the government to regulate media violence, critics say that in practical terms it would be impossible. They point out that the government would have to come up with a meaningful way to define violence, and then it would have to decide how much violence is too much. As vice president of the First Amendment Center Gene Policinski argues, this would be difficult:

> I suspect most agree that torture and bloody carnage are at one end of the socially acceptable spectrum of violent scenes and that purely slapstick . . . kinds of comedic brutality are

Critics contend that parental supervision is not enough to prevent children's exposure to violent media.

at the other. But where on the culture meter should a government body put those popular faux-documentary programs where real police officers are shown using brute force in making actual arrests? . . . And what about blood-and-bash reality shows that purport to be full-contact "sports" events, or professional boxing matches? What about war movies—to say nothing of the real war images from Iraq, Afghanistan and elsewhere? . . . well, you get the idea, and perhaps a sense of the difficulty.[74]

Yet despite such difficulties, proponents of regulation say it can be done. In its 2007 report the FCC finds that "while there are legal, evidentiary, analytical, and social science obstacles that need to be overcome in defining harmful violence [for the purpose of regulation], Congress likely has the ability and authority to craft a sustainable definition."[75]

The V-Chip and Television Ratings

Many people say the V-chip and television rating systems are the best ways for individuals to screen media violence that bothers them. In January 1996 the FCC mandated that every television 13 inches and larger manufactured after 2000 contain the V-chip. This chip works in conjunction with the TV Parental Guidelines and allows the user to screen content by the ratings of the programs. Many cable and satellite boxes also have similar parental controls. According to McDowell, "Today's parents have at their disposal more choices in parental controls and blocking technologies than ever before. Never have parents been more empowered to choose what their children should and should not watch."[76] While some people argue that these parental controls are not effective, others contend that the problem is that people do not know how to use them or simply choose not to.

> " Even if the majority of society decided that it was desirable for the government to regulate media violence, critics say that in practical terms it would be impossible. "

Others insist that the V-chip and similar technologies do not work. In its 2007 report the FCC finds that "Although the V-chip and TV ratings system appear useful in the abstract, they are not effective at protecting children from violent content."[77] The Parents Television Council also believes that the V-chip is not a good solution. V-chip technology uses content descriptors of the programming. However, the organization finds that, "every broadcast network has had problems with the accurate and consistent application of content descriptors. . . . Content descriptors are not being used on the vast majority of general audience shows containing sex, violence, or adult language."[78]

The Role of the First Amendment

Many people believe that any restriction of media violence would violate the First Amendment, which protects freedom of expression. The ACLU maintains, "The Supreme Court has repeatedly stressed that 'above all else, the First Amendment means that government has no power to restrict expression because of its message, its ideas, its subject matter, or its content.'"[79] Any media content restrictions must promote a compelling government interest, says the ACLU, but argues that violence has not been proven to cause lasting harm and is thus not a compelling interest. Clay Calvert, co-director of the Pennsylvania Center for the First Amendment at Pennsylvania State University, concludes, "There is very little chance that a bill attempting to define violence and regulate it would ever pass constitutional muster."[80] Yet some people believe that like the harmful impact of indecency, violence also poses enough of a threat to deserve some government regulation.

> " **Many people believe that any restriction of media violence would violate the First Amendment.** "

Industry Regulation

At present, media violence is largely self-regulated by the media industry, yet people disagree over whether this is effective. Some critics charge that problems associated with media violence could be reduced if the industry better regulated itself. In the opinion of scholar Rhoda Rabkin, while industry regulation might not be perfect, it is still the best option. She says, "The expansion of the federal government's regulatory powers in the area of entertainment and culture is undesirable compared to the traditional, and still workable, system of industry self-censorship."[81] Others contend that the industry is simply not responsible enough to effectively regulate media violence. Says FCC commissioner Michael J. Copps:

> Industry's efforts have obviously not solved the problem and the preoccupation of some media—especially large national conglomerates often more interested in selling products to young people than in removing violence

from the airwaves—does not provide much confidence that it will move to solve the problem.[82]

Public Opinion

Surveys of public opinion show that a majority of the public is concerned with media violence, yet most people believe that parents, not government, are the solution to problems related to media violence. In a 2005 survey the Pew Research Center found that 79 percent of people believe inadequate parental supervision rather than inadequate laws is responsible for children being exposed to offensive media material such as graphic violence. Of those surveyed, 86 percent believed that parents, not the entertainment industry, are responsible for protecting children from violence on television and in movies. Only about a third believe government regulations and fines are the best way to curb violence in the media. Another survey, conducted in 2006 by Russell Research, showed similar results. Of those surveyed, 82 percent believed individuals should exercise personal choice over the media content they consume, and only 12 percent preferred government regulation. More than three-quarters of those surveyed said they would be upset if government regulation limited their media content choices.

> Some critics charge that problems associated with media violence could be reduced if the industry better regulated itself.

Marjorie Heins, founder of the Free Expression Policy Project says, "In the end . . . violent entertainment will probably never be squelched. One of the ironies of media-violence politics is that despite the periodic brouhaha, not many viewers would willingly give up their favorite . . . shows, horror movies, bruising sports events, or action-hero extravaganzas."[83] In this society where a continued presence of media violence exists, so does the continued disagreement about how best to solve it. Critics argue over the effectiveness of reducing overall media violence, parental supervision, government regulation, V-chip and television ratings, and industry self-regulation.

How Can the Problems Associated with Media Violence Be Reduced?

66The volume and degree of violence on broadcast television must be reduced, especially during the times of day when children compose a significant portion of the viewing audience.99

—Tim Winter, "A Commentary on the Federal Communications Commission Report," First Amendment Center, April 27, 2007. www.firstamendmentcenter.org.

Winter is president of the Parents Television Council, an organization dedicated to improving the quality of television content.

66The solution [to problems caused by media violence] does not lie in simply reducing the amount.99

—W. James Potter, *The 11 Myths of Media Violence.* Thousand Oaks, CA: Sage, 2003, p. 140.

Potter is a professor, author of numerous books, and has served on the editorial boards and as a reviewer for a number of journals.

Bracketed quotes indicate conflicting positions.

* Editor's Note: While the definition of a primary source can be narrowly or broadly defined, for the purposes of Compact Research, a primary source consists of: 1) results of original research presented by an organization or researcher; 2) eyewitness accounts of events, personal experience, or work experience; 3) first-person editorials offering pundits' opinions; 4) government officials presenting political plans and/or policies; 5) representatives of organizations presenting testimony or policy.

> **❝The ultimate filter is the on/off switch, which not only shields children from violent programming but tells networks and advertisers to offer different fare.❞**

—*Los Angeles Times*, "Let Parents Handle TV Violence," April 27, 2007. www.latimes.com.

The *Los Angeles Times* is a daily newspaper.

> **❝I continue to believe that . . . industry self-regulation is preferable to direct governmental intervention.❞**

—George Ivie, "Hearing on Television Ratings Accuracy and the FAIR Ratings Bill," testimony before the U.S. Senate Committee on Commerce, Science and Transportation, July 27, 2005.

Ivie is executive director of the Media Rating Council, an organization that sets rating standards for the media industry.

> **❝While I support self-regulation first, these discussions [about the problem of media violence] have been going on for far too long. It is time that more effective steps are taken to protect our children.❞**

—Deborah Taylor Tate, statement regarding "Violent Television Programming and Its Impact on Children," Federal Communications Commission, April 6, 2007.

Tate is a commissioner for the Federal Communications Commission, a government agency with the primary goal of protecting American consumers.

> **❝As an American, I absolutely refuse to have my private entertainment dictated to me. . . . That's what the Founding Fathers fought for, and that is one of the core freedoms we fight for to this very day—the right to watch whatever trash I want to.❞**

—Amanda Pandagon, "The C***** C****d*** on Ind******," *Pandagon*, August 30, 2005. http://pandagon.net.

Pandagon writes for the *Pandagon* Web site.

"Parents have the power to regulate the media in their lives and the lives of their children."

—Adam Thierer, "The Right Way to Regulate Violent TV," Progress & Freedom Foundation, May 2007. www.pff.org.

Thierer is director of the Center for Digital Media Freedom and former director of telecommunications at the Cato Institute.

"As parents and guardians . . . we can limit . . . our children's access to media violence. But none of us can solve it alone or just as parents. . . . It has gone way beyond that."

—Michael J. Copps, remarks to the Parents Television Council, Washington, D.C., January 10, 2007.

Copps is a commissioner for the Federal Communications Commission, a government agency with the primary goal of protecting American consumers.

"Given the tools parents have to filter what their children see, including the V-chip, ratings from producers and independent groups, and cable and satellite system controls, the excuse for regulating content on *any* channel is weaker than ever."

—Jacob Sullum, "The Mystery of Violence," *Reason*, May 16, 2007. www.reason.com.

Sullum is senior editor *of Reason* magazine and writes a weekly column that appears in a number of newspapers including the *New York Post* and the *Washington Times*.

"Current blocking technologies and ratings systems are insufficient. . . . Less than half of the TV sets in American households are capable of blocking content that is not suitable for children. Even parents who have TVs equipped with a V-chip need more help."

—Kevin J. Martin, statement regarding "Violent Television Programming and Its Impact on Children," Federal Communications Commission, April 6, 2007. www.fcc.gov.

Martin is chairman of the Federal Communications Commission, a government agency with the primary goal of protecting American consumers.

❝The government should not replace parents as decision makers in America's living rooms. There are some things the government does well, but deciding what is aired and when on television is not one of them.❞

—Caroline Fredrickson, "ACLU Calls FCC Television Violence Recommendations Unworkable," American Civil Liberties Union, press release, April 26, 2007. www.aclu.org.

Fredrickson is director of the American Civil Liberties Union Washington Legislative Office.

❝We recognize that violent content is a protected form of speech under the First Amendment, but . . . government interests at stake, such as protecting children from excessively violent television programming [may] . . . justify . . . content-based regulations.❞

—Federal Communications Commission, "Violent Television Programming and Its Impact on Children," April 6, 2007. www.fcc.gov.

The Federal Communications Commission is a government agency with the primary goal of protecting American consumers.

❝Media violence is not the sole or even the most important factor in youth violence. Thus, there is no compelling government interest in regulating such content.❞

—American Civil Liberties Union, "ACLU Comments to the Federal Communications Commission re: MB Docket No. 04-261, the Matter of Violent Television Programming and Its Impact on Children," September 15, 2004. www.aclu.org.

The American Civil Liberties Union was founded to help protect individual rights, including freedom of speech and of the press, in the United States.

"Any direct regulation of violent themes and images on cable television would constitute a content-based regulation of high value speech in violation of the First Amendment."

—Geoffrey R. Stone, "The First Amendment Implications of Government Regulation of 'Violent' Programming on Cable Television," National Cable & Telecommunications Association, October 15, 2004. www.ncta.com.

Stone is a law professor at the University of Chicago and author of *Perilous Times: Free Speech in Wartime.*

"Any trend to produce programmes and products . . . which in the name of entertainment exalt violence . . . is a perversion. . . . I appeal to the leaders of the media industry to educate and encourage producers to safeguard the common good, to uphold the truth, to protect individual human dignity and promote respect for the needs of the family."

—Benedict XVI, "Children and the Media: a Challenge for Education," message from the Vatican, January 24, 2007.

Benedict XVI is the two hundred sixty-fifth pope and head of the Roman Catholic Church.

How Can the Problems Associated with Media Violence Be Reduced?

- The Kaiser Family Foundation reports that nearly **66 percent** television programs contain violence.

- According to the organization ACT Against Violence, **15 percent** of all U.S. television programs per week contain violence, the highest percentage of any nation in the world.

- According to the organization TV Watch, **68 percent** of America's television-viewing households do not include children under **age 18**.

- In a 2005 survey of **1,505 Americans**, the Pew Research Center found that **86 percent** of people believed parents, rather than the entertainment industry, are responsible for keeping children from viewing media violence.

- In a 2006 survey of **501 registered voters**, Russell Research found that only **12 percent** of people wanted increased government regulation of television content.

- In a 2007 survey of **1,008 parents**, the Kaiser Family Foundation found that of those parents who had heard of the television rating system, only **51 percent** knew that "V" stands for violent content.

Violence on Television Has Increased

This chart shows that violence on prime-time broadcast television during the 9:00 PM hour has increased compared to 1998 levels. Between 2005 and 2006 it increased significantly on every channel studied, except the Fox and NBC networks.

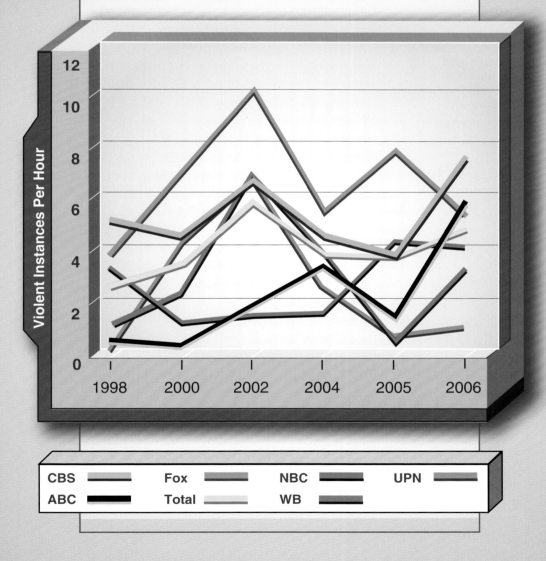

CBS   Fox   NBC   UPN

ABC   Total   WB

Source: Parents Television Council, "Dying to Entertain: Violence on Prime Time Broadcast Television 1998 to 2006," January 2007. www.parentstv.org.

85

Majority of Parents Say They Monitor Children's Media Use

Data from a Kaiser Family Foundation survey reveal that the majority of parents say they closely monitor their children's media use. Only 18 percent of those surveyed believe they should do more to monitor that use.

Percent of parents who say they...

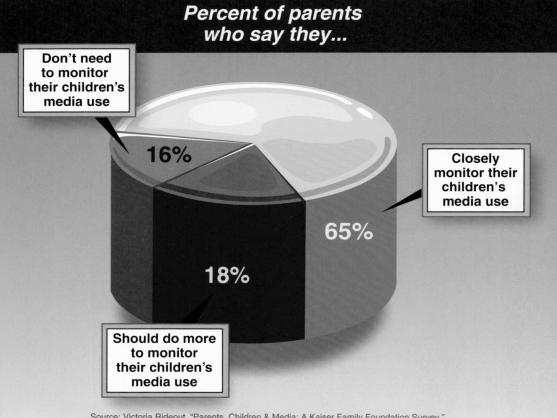

Don't need to monitor their children's media use

16%

Closely monitor their children's media use

65%

18%

Should do more to monitor their children's media use

Source: Victoria Rideout, "Parents, Children & Media: A Kaiser Family Foundation Survey," *Kaiser Family Foundation*, June 2007. www.kff.org.

• According to the Web site *Turn Off Your TV*, only **10 percent** of children's viewing time is spent watching children's television; the other **90 percent** is spent watching programs designed for adults.

Limited Support for Increased Government Regulation

Data from a 2005 Pew Research Center survey show that more Americans see danger in government restriction of media than in harmful content. Half of those surveyed believe that the audience is responsible for avoiding violent content and more people favor public boycotts of violent material than government regulation.

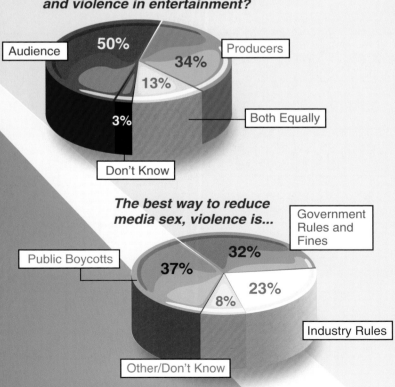

What is a greater danger?

Don't Know

11%

41%   48%

Harmful Content   Undue Government Restrictions

Who should be responsible for sex and violence in entertainment?

Audience   50%   Producers

34%

13%

3%   Both Equally

Don't Know

The best way to reduce media sex, violence is...

Public Boycotts   Government Rules and Fines

37%   32%

8%   23%

Other/Don't Know   Industry Rules

Source: Pew Research Center, "Support for Tougher Indecency Measures, but Worries About Government Intrusiveness," April 19, 2005. www.people-press.org.

Most Parents Are Satisfied with Blocking Tools

According to the results of this survey conducted by TV Watch, 83 percent of parents are satisfied with the effectiveness of the V-chip or other available blocking tools in limiting media content they believe is inappropriate for their children.

How satisfied are you with the effectiveness of the V-chip or other blocking tools available in your home in limiting television programming you find inappropriate for your children?

Total	Kids 0–5	Kids 6–10	Kids 11–13	Kids 14–18	
43%	37%	48%	38%	44%	Very Satisfied
40%	48%	39%	40%	37%	Somewhat Satisfied
5%	1%	6%	8%	5%	Somewhat dissatisfied
3%	1%	3%	4%	4%	Very Dissatisfied
9%	12%	4%	10%	11%	Don't Know/ Refused

Source: Hart Research, "TV Watch Survey of Parents Topline," *TV Watch*, June 2007. www.televisionwatch.org.

- Russell Research reports that **85 percent** of parents find television ratings useful.

- A 2005 survey commissioned by the National Center for Missing & Exploited Children and Cox Communications reveals that while nearly **50 percent** of the parents surveyed monitor their children's online activity daily or weekly, the other **50 percent** admitted they did not even know that such monitoring tools are available.

Key People and Advocacy Groups

Mitch Bainwol: Bainwol is the chairman and chief executive officer of the Recording Industry Association of America, a trade group that represents the recording industry in the United States and is responsible for the voluntary Parental Advisory label on music that contains violent lyrics.

Caroline Fredrickson: Fredrickson is director of the American Civil Liberties Union (ACLU) Washington Legislative Office. The ACLU was founded to help protect individual rights, including freedom of speech and of the press, in the United States.

Joan Graves: Graves is chairman of the Classification and Ratings Administration of the Motion Picture Association of America (MPAA), the body that rates motion pictures in the United States.

Marjorie Heins: Heins is founder of the Free Expression Policy Project. She is opposed to restrictions on violent media content.

Kevin J. Martin: Martin is chairman of the Federal Communications Commission (FCC), a government agency with the primary goal of protecting American consumers.

Jeff McIntyre: McIntyre is an expert on the effects of media on youth and is the senior legislative and federal affairs officer for the American Psychological Association, an organization that works to promote health, education, and human welfare in the United States.

Kyle McSlarrow: McSlarrow is president of the National Cable & Telecommunications Association, a trade association that represents more than 200 cable program networks.

Gene Policinski: Policinski is vice president and executive director of the First Amendment Center, an organization that works to protect First Amendment freedoms such as freedom of speech.

Victoria Rideout: Rideout is vice president of the Kaiser Family Foundation, an organization that focuses on major health issues affecting the United States, including the effects of media violence.

Adam Thierer: Thierer is director of the Center for Digital Media Freedom. He is opposed to censorship of media violence.

Patricia Vance: Vance is president of the Entertainment Software Rating Board, which rates video games in the United States.

David Walsh: David Walsh is president and founder of the National Institute on Media and the Family, a nonprofit organization that conducts research and provides information for parents about the impact of the media on children and families.

Tim Winter: Tim Winter is president of the Parents Television Council, an organization founded with the goal of preventing children's media exposure to sex, violence, and profanity.

Chronology

1908

Police in Chicago refuse to provide a permit for the public display of the movie *The James Boys in Missouri*, because its content includes depictions of violent lawbreaking.

1984

The Attorney General Task Force on Family Violence finds that there is overwhelming evidence that television violence contributes to real violence.

1933–1935

The Payne Fund studies conclude that violent motion pictures can directly influence youth to become juvenile delinquents and criminals.

1982

A study by the National Institutes of Mental Health mentions a link between television violence and aggression.

1900   1910   1920   1930   1940   1950   1960   1970   1980

1920s

As the popularity of movies grows, there is increasing public pressure on the movie industry to do something about what many people believe to be excessive violence in movies.

1952

The first congressional hearings are held on violence in radio and television and its impact on youth.

1972

A report by the U.S. surgeon general cites evidence of a link between television violence and aggressive behavior.

1947

In response to public concerns about violent comic book content, the industry establishes the Association of Comic Magazine Publishers. In the 1950s the association creates a code banning torture, sadism, and detailed descriptions of criminal acts.

1961

The results of the first major investigation of the effects of television on children in North America are published. Researchers find the content of television to be extremely violent, but caution that television is, at most, a contributing factor in causing violent and delinquent behaviors.

1986

America's motion picture industry adopts its voluntary film rating system in response to public demand for some kind of regulation of film content.

2000

The Federal Trade Commission releases a report showing how media industries, including the music industry, aggressively market media meant for adults to young children. The V-chip, used to block television programs based on their ratings, is required in all televisions 13 inches or larger.

1990

The Recording Industry Association of America creates a standardized Parental Advisory label, a voluntary warning label for audio and video music recordings containing explicit lyrics including depictions of violence and sex.

1985   1990   1995   2000   2005

1994

The Entertainment Software Rating Board is established by the Entertainment Software Association to assign computer and video game content ratings and enforce industry-adopted advertising guidelines.

1999

In Littleton, Colorado, high school students Eric Harris and Dylan Klebold open fire in Columbine High School, killing a teacher and 14 students—including themselves—and injuring 28 others. The incident spawns a national debate on the effect of media violence on youth.

2007

The Federal Communications Commission releases a report suggesting that Congress consider regulations that would restrict violent media content on television in order to protect children.

1996

Rap singer Tupac Shakur is shot dead, causing many people to question the effect of violent music lyrics.

1997

The television rating system debuts on cable stations and broadcast networks.

1998

Violent video game *Grand Theft Auto* incites heated controversy concerning violent video games and their effect on youth.

Related Organizations

Center for Creative Voices in Media

1220 L St. NW, Suite 100–494

Washington, DC 20005

phone: (202) 747-1712 • fax: (202) 318-9183

e-mail: info@creativevoices.us • Web site: www.creativevoices.us

The Center for Creative Voices in Media is a nonprofit organization dedicated to preserving diversity in America's media. The organization believes that American culture depends on the free expression of ideas. It opposes any government censorship of media content—including censorship to protect children—because it believes this stifles diversity and violates the First Amendment.

Center for Media Literacy

23852 Pacific Coast Hwy., #472

Malibu, CA 90265

phone: (310) 456-1225 • fax: (310) 456-0020

e-mail: cml@medialit.org • Web site: www.medialit.org

This nonprofit national educational organization promotes media literacy as a way to help youth develop critical-thinking skills and to analyze media content. It believes that rather than simply trying to place blame for the negative effects of media violence, society needs to begin discussing this topic in new ways. Its Web site features articles and reports about media literacy.

Entertainment Software Rating Board (ESRB)

317 Madison Ave., 22nd Floor

New York, NY 10017

Web site: www.esrb.org

The ESRB is a nonprofit, self-regulatory body established in 1994 by the Entertainment Software Association. It assigns computer and video game content ratings, enforces industry-adopted advertising guidelines, and helps ensure responsible online privacy practices for the interactive entertainment software industry.

Federal Communications Commission (FCC)

445 12th St. SW

Washington, DC 20554

phone: (888) 225-5322 • fax: (866) 418-0230

e-mail: fccinfo@fcc.gov • Web site: www.fcc.gov

The Federal Communications Commission (FCC) is an independent U.S. government agency that was established by the Communications Act of 1934. It is charged with regulating interstate and international communications by radio, television, wire, satellite, and cable.

Free Expression Policy Project (FEPP)

170 West 76th St., #301

New York, NY 10023

e-mail: margeheins@verizon.net • Web site: www.fepproject.org

The Free Expression Policy Project provides research and advocacy on issues concerning free speech and the media. It believes that sexual and racial harassment, threats, and false advertising are types of speech that do not, and should not, have First Amendment protection. But it is opposed to the censorship of any content that does not have a direct, tangible, and demonstrably harmful effect. It does not support censorship designed to protect youth from controversial media content.

Media Awareness Network (MNet)

1500 Merivale Rd., 3rd Floor

Ottawa, Ontario, Canada K2E 6Z5

phone: (613) 224-7721 • fax: (613) 224-1958

e-mail: info@media-awareness.ca • Web site: www.media-awareness.ca

The Media Awareness Network is a nonprofit Canadian organization that promotes media education and Internet literacy for both children and adults. It provides a collection of reference materials for various age groups in order to help them examine media issues.

Morality in Media

475 Riverside Dr., Suite 239

New York, NY 10115

phone: (212) 870-3222 • fax: (212) 870-2765

e-mail: mim@moralityinmedia.org

Web site: www.moralityinmedia.org

Morality in Media is a nonprofit organization that was originally established to combat pornography. It works to inform citizens and public officials about the harms of pornography, obscenity, and violence in the media and about what they can do through the law to protect their communities and children. It maintains the National Obscenity Law Center, a clearinghouse of legal materials on obscenity law, and conducts public information programs to educate and involve concerned citizens.

National Coalition Against Censorship (NCAC)

275 Seventh Ave.

New York, NY 10001

phone: (212) 807-6222 • fax: (212) 807-6245

e-mail: ncac@ncac.org • Web site: www.ncac.org

The NCAC is an alliance of 50 national nonprofit organizations, including artistic, religious, educational, professional, and civil liberties groups. It works to promote and defend freedom of thought, inquiry, and expression and opposes media restriction.

National Institute on Media and the Family

606 24th Ave. South, Suite 606

Minneapolis, MN 55454

phone: (888) 672-5427 • fax: (612) 672-4113

Web site: www.mediafamily.org

The National Institute on Media and the Family is a nonprofit organization that works to maximize the benefits and minimize the harm of media on children. It conducts research and functions as an international resource center to help educate families about their media choices.

Parents Television Council (PTC)

707 Wilshire Blvd., Suite 2075

Los Angeles, CA 90017

phone: (213) 629-9255

Web site: www.parentstv.org

The Parents Television Council was founded in 1995 with the goal of reducing children's exposure to violence, sex, and profanity in the media. It has nearly 1 million members across the United States and works with television producers, broadcasters, networks, and sponsors in an effort to stem the flow of harmful and negative messages targeted to children. PTC has produced numerous research reports documenting the increase of violence, sex, and profanity in the media.

For Further Research

Books

Craig A. Anderson, Douglas A. Gentile, and Katherine E. Buckley, *Violent Video Game Effects on Children and Adolescents: Theory, Research, and Public Policy.* New York: Oxford University Press, 2007.

Karen Boyle, *Media and Violence: Gendering the Debates.* Thousand Oaks, CA: Sage, 2005.

Cynthia Carter and C. Kay Weaver, *Violence and the Media.* Philadelphia: Open University Press, 2003.

Nancy E. Dowd, Dorothy G. Singer, and Robin Fret, eds., *Handbook of Children, Culture, and Violence.* Thousand Oaks, CA: Sage, 2003.

Gerard Jones, *Killing Monsters: Why Children Need Fantasy, Super Heroes, and Make-Believe Violence.* New York: Basic Books, 2002.

Steven J. Kirsh, *Children, Adolescents, and Media Violence: A Critical Look at the Research.* Thousand Oaks, CA: Sage, 2006.

W. James Potter, *The 11 Myths of Media Violence.* Thousand Oaks, CA: Sage, 2003.

Diane Ravitch and Joseph P. Viteritti, eds., *Kid Stuff: Marketing Sex and Violence to America's Children.* Baltimore: Johns Hopkins University Press, 2003.

David Trend, *The Myth of Media Violence.* Malden, MA: Blackwell, 2007.

C. Kay Weaver and Cynthia Carter, eds., *Critical Readings: Violence and the Media.* New York: Open University Press, 2006.

Periodicals

Debashis Aikat, "Streaming Violent Genres Online: Visual Images in Music Videos on BET.com, Country.com, MTV.com, VH1.com," *Popular Music and Society*, June 2004.

Lilian R. BeVier, "Controlling Communications That Teach or Demonstrate Violence: 'The Movie Made Them Do It,'" *Journal of Law, Medicine, & Ethics*, Spring 2004.

Tina L. Cheng et al., "Children's Violent Television Viewing: Are Parents Monitoring?" *Pediatrics*, July 2004.

Christian Science Monitor, "The Media Industry Has Not Self-Regulated to the Satisfaction of Parents. The Government Should Step In," May 10, 2007.

Anne-Marie Cusac, "Watching Torture in Prime Time," *Progressive*, August 2005.

John Eggerton, "Violence: The New Indecency?" *Broadcasting & Cable*, January 22, 2007.

Robert K. Goidel, Craig M. Freeman, and Steven T. Procopio, "The Impact of Television Viewing on Perceptions of Juvenile Crime," *Journal of Broadcasting & Electronic Media*, March 2006.

Jennifer Harper, "Film Ratings for Violence Labeled as Meaningless," *Washington Times*, May 3, 2005.

David Hoppe, "Hiding Behind the First Amendment," *Nuvo*, May 2, 2007.

Kerry Howley, "Parents Adrift on an Angry Sea," *Reason*, April 27, 2007.

Seth Killian, "Violent Video Game Players Mysteriously Avoid Killing Selves, Others," *NCAC Censorship News*, Winter 2003/2004.

Los Angeles Times, "Let Parents Handle TV Violence," April 27, 2007.

Paul McMasters, "The Games Censors Play," *North Country Gazette*, October 19, 2006.

Kim Newman, "Torture Garden," *Sight and Sound*, June 2006.

New Scientist, "In Denial: Why Are We So Reluctant to Accept That On-Screen Violence Is Bad for Us?" April 21, 2007.

Amanda Paulson, "Defining Violence Narrowly Enough to Satisfy the Courts Is a Tricky Challenge for Congress," *Christian Science Monitor*, April 30, 2007.

Richard Sambrook, "Regulation, Responsibility and the Case Against Censorship," *Index on Censorship*, January 2006.

Jacob Sullum, "The Mystery of Violence," *Reason*, May 16, 2007.

Adam Thierer, "Natural Born Regulators," *National Review*, March 29, 2006.

Clive Thomson, "You Grew Up Playing Shoot'em-Up Games. Why Can't Your Kids?" *Wired*, April 9, 2007.

Cynthia G. Wagner, "Aggression and Violent Media: Playing Video Games May Lead to More Violence than Watching TV," *Futurist*, July/August 2004.

Daphne White, "Trapped in the Matrix of Unreal Ratings Systems," *Washington Post*, May 25, 2003.

Internet Sources

Federal Communications Commission, "Violent Television Programming and Its Impact on Children," April 6, 2007. http://hraunfoss. fcc.gov/edocs_public/attachmatch/FCC-07-50A1.pdf.

Free Expression Policy Project, "Fact Sheet: Media Violence," January 2004. www.fepproject.org/factsheets/mediaviolence.html.

Jonathan L. Freedman, "Television Violence and Aggression: Setting the Record Straight," *Media Institute*, May 2007. www.mediainstitute.org/ issue_papers/policyviews/2007/Freedman-TelevisionViolence.pdf.

National Institute on Media and the Family, "11th Annual MediaWise Video Game Report Card," November 28, 2006. www. mediafamily. org/research/report_vgrc_2006.shtml.

———, "Fact Sheet: Children and Media Violence," November 2006. www.mediafamily.org/facts/facts_vlent.shtml.

Parents Television Council, "Dying to Entertain: Violence on Prime Time Broadcast Television 1998 to 2006," January 2007. www.parentstv. org/PTC/publications/reports/violencestudy/DyingtoEntertain.pdf.

Donald F. Roberts, Ulla G. Foehr, and Victoria Rideout, "Generation M: Media in the Lives of 8-18-Year-Olds," *Kaiser Family Foundation*, March 2005. www.kff.org/entmedia/upload/Generation-M-Media-in-the-Lives-of-8-18-Year-olds-Report.pdf.

Source Notes

Overview

1. Federal Communications Commission, "Violent Television Programming and Its Impact on Children," April 6, 2007. www.fcc.gov.
2. David Walsh, "Kilographic Entertainment," *National Institute on Media and the Family*. www.mediafamily.org.
3. Parents Television Council, "Dying to Entertain: Violence on Prime Time Broadcast Television 1998 to 2006," January 2007. www.parentstv.org.
4. Rachel Halliburton, "Teenage Cults: Blood and Gore on the Web," *New Statesman*, March 28, 2005.
5. Jonathan L. Freedman "No Real Evidence for TV Violence Causing Real Violence," *First Amendment Center*, April 27, 2007. www.firstamendmentcenter.org.
6. Miriam Gross, "Putting a Stop to Media Violence," *Spectator*, December 9, 2006.
7. Henry Jenkins, "A Few Thoughts on Media Violence," 2007. www.henryjenkins.org.
8. David Hoppe, "Hiding Behind the First Amendment," *Nuvo*, May 2, 2007. www.nuvo.net.
9. Kevin W. Saunders, "Media Industry Should Take FCC Report Seriously," *First Amendment Center*, April 27, 2007. www.firstamendmentcenter.org.
10. Free Expression Policy Project, "Fact Sheet: Media Violence," January 2004. www.fepproject.org.
11. American Civil Liberties Union, "ACLU Comments to the Federal Communications Commission re: MB Docket No. 04-261, the Matter of Violent Television Programming and Its Impact on Children," September 15, 2004. www.aclu.org.
12. Adam Thierer, "Natural Born Regulators," *National Review*, March 29, 2006. www.nationalreview.com.
13. National Institute on Media and the Family, "11th Annual MediaWise Video Game Report Card," November 28, 2006. www.mediafamily.org.
14. Hoppe, "Hiding Behind the First Amendment."
15. Kyle McSlarrow, "Images Children See on the Screen," testimony before the U.S. House of Representatives Subcommittee on Telecommunications and the Internet, Washington D.C., June 22, 2007.
16. American Civil Liberties Union, "What Is Censorship?" www.aclu.org.
17. American Civil Liberties Union, "What Is Censorship?"
18. American Civil Liberties Union, "What Is Censorship?"
19. Federal Communications Commission, "Violent Television Programming."
20. W. James Potter, *The 11 Myths of Media Violence*. Thousand Oaks, CA: Sage, 2003, p. 1.

How Does Media Violence Affect Society?

21. Paul K. McMasters, "Watch Out for Studies About TV Harming Kids," *North Country Gazette*, May 4, 2006. www.northcountrygazette.org.
22. McMasters, "Watch Out for Studies."
23. National Institute on Media and the Family, "Fact Sheet: Children and Media Violence," November 2006. www.mediafamily.org.
24. Freedman, "No Real Evidence for TV Violence Causing Real Violence."

25. Free Expression Policy Project, "Fact Sheet: Media Violence."

26. Potter, *The 11 Myths of Media Violence*, p. 2.

27. Jonathan L. Freedman, *Media Violence and Its Effect on Aggression: Assessing the Scientific Evidence.* Toronto: University of Toronto Press, 2002, p. 6.

28. Jonathan L. Freedman, "Television Violence and Aggression: Setting the Record Straight," Media Institute, May 2007. www.mediainstitute.org.

29. Jeff McIntyre, testimony before the U.S. House of Representatives Committee on the Judiciary, Subcommittee on the Courts, the Internet, and Intellectual Property, Washington, D.C., May 20, 2004.

30. Potter, *The 11 Myths of Media Violence*, pp. xv–xvi.

31. Shannon Young, "A Dangerous Thing: The Debate over TV Violence," *Australian Screen Education*, Autumn 2004.

32. Healthy Minds, "Psychiatric Effects of Media Violence." www.healthyminds.org.

33. Tim Winter, "A Commentary on the Federal Communications Commission Report," First Amendment Center, April 27, 2007. www.firstamendmentcenter.org.

34. Potter, *The 11 Myths of Media Violence*, p. 83.

35. Marjorie Heins, "Bleep: Censoring Hollywood?" remarks to the National Press Club, April 18, 2005.

36. Quoted in Mark Stackpole, "Crash! Boom! Bang! Does TV Violence Affect Our Children?" iParenting, Preschool and Child Channel, http://children-today.com.

37. Cynthia Carter and C. Kay Weaver, *Violence and the Media.* Philadelphia: Open University Press, 2003, p. 16.

Do Violent Video Games Inspire Violence?

38. Craig Anderson, "The Research Is In: Violent Video Games Can Lead to Violent Behavior," *Executive Intelligence Review*, June 1, 2007. www.larouchepub.com.

39. Seth Killian, "Violent Video Game Players Mysteriously Avoid Killing Selves, Others," *NCAC Censorship News*, Winter 2003/2004. www.ncac.org.

40. Duke Ferris, "The Truth About Violent Youth and Video Games," *Game Daily*, October 11, 2005. http://biz.gamedaily.com.

41. Anderson, "The Research Is In."

42. Quoted in Emily Halevy and Yvette Brown, "Violence and Video Games," Connect with Kids, May 9, 2007. www.connectwithkids.com.

43. Duke Ferris, "Caution: Children at Play: The Truth About Violent Youth and Video Games," *Game Revolution*, October 19, 2005. www.gamerevolution.com.

44. U.S. District Court for the District of Minnesota, *ESA et al. v. Hatch et al.*, July 2006.

45. Neil Gerstein, "Do Video Games Lead to Violence or Not?" *Ezine Articles.com*, May 25, 2007. http://ezinearticles.com.

46. Quoted in Arlen Panchoo, "Impact of Video Game Realism," *New Media Journalism*, December 7, 2006. www.fims.uwo.ca.

47. Jonathan Harbour, "The ESRB Rating System: A Gamer's Perspective," July 15, 2006. http://theharbourfamily.com.

48. Mickey Suhn Lee, "Effects of Video Game Violence on Prosocial and Antisocial Behaviors," *Journal of Young Investigators*, August 2004.

49. Thierer, "Natural Born Regulators."

50. Daphne White, "Trapped in the Matrix of Unreal Ratings Systems," *Washington Post*, May 25, 2003. www.washingtonpost.com.

51. Anderson, "The Research Is In."

Is Current Regulation of Media Violence Effective?

52. Quoted in First Amendment Center, "Movie Ratings Board Invites Scrutiny," January 25, 2006. www.firstamendmentcenter.org.

53. Motion Picture Association of America, "Frequently Asked Questions." www.mpaa.org.

54. Quoted in Jennifer Harper, "Film Ratings for Violence Labeled as Meaningless," *Washington Times*, May 3, 2005. www.washingtontimes.com.

55. McSlarrow, "Images Children See on the Screen."

56. Deborah Taylor Tate, statement regarding "Violent Television Programming and Its Impact on Children," Federal Communications Commission, April 6, 2007. www.fcc.gov.

57. Hillary Rodham Clinton, interview with GameCore, "Senator Clinton on Violent Games," *CBS News*, August 5, 2005. www.cbsnews.com.

58. Thierer, "Natural Born Regulators."

59. Entertainment Software Association, "Games and Violence." www.theesa.com.

60. COPA Commission, "Internet Filter Effectiveness: Testing Over- and Underinclusive Blocking Decisions of Four Popular Filters." www.copacommission.org.

61. Quoted in Recording Industry Association of America, "Parental Advisory." www.riaa.com.

62. Adam Thierer, "The Right Way to Regulate Violent TV," Progress & Freedom Foundation, May 2007. www.pff.org.

63. Thierer, "The Right Way to Regulate Violent TV."

64. Peter Suderman, "Gaming the System," *National Review*, May 1, 2007. www.nationalreview.com.

65. Hillary Rodham Clinton, "Senator Clinton's Speech to Kaiser Family Foundation upon Release of *Generation M: Media in the Lives of Kids 8 to 18*," March 8, 2005. http://clinton.senate.gov.

How Can the Problems Associated with Media Violence Be Reduced?

66. Robert M. McDowell, statement regarding "Violent Television Programming and Its Impact on Children," Federal Communications Commission, April 6, 2007. www.fcc.gov.

67. Thierer, "The Right Way to Regulate Violent TV."

68. McDowell, statement regarding "Violent Television Programming."

69. Adam D. Thierer, "Desperate Housewives and Desperate Regulators," *Cato Institute*, January 4, 2005. www.cato.org.

70. *Christian Science Monitor*, "The Media Industry Has Not Self-Regulated to the Satisfaction of Parents. The Government Should Step In," May 10, 2007. www.csmonitor.com.

71. Jonathan S. Adelstein, statement regarding "Violent Television Programming and Its Impact on Children," Federal Communications Commission, April 6, 2007. www.fcc.gov.

72. Quoted in Amanda Paulson, "Defining Violence Narrowly Enough to Satisfy Courts Is a Tricky Challenge for Congress," *Christian Science Monitor*, April 30, 2007. www.csmonitor.com.

73. Caroline Fredrickson, "ACLU Calls FCC Television Violence Recommendations Unworkable," American Civil Liberties Union, press release, April

26, 2007. www.aclu.org.

74. Gene Policinski, "TV Violence: More Program Information Would Be Better than Regulation," *National Newspaper Association*, May 3, 2007. http://www.nna.org.

75. Federal Communications Commission, "Violent Television Programming."

76. McDowell, statement regarding "Violent Television Programming."

77. Federal Communications Commission, "Violent Television Programming."

78. Parents Television Council, "Dying to Entertain."

79. American Civil Liberties Union, "ACLU Comments to the Federal Communications Commission."

80. Quoted in Paulson, "Defining Violence Narrowly."

81. Rhoda Rabkin, "Do Kids Need Government Censors?" *Policy Review*, February/March 2002. www.hoover.org.

82. Michael J. Copps, statement regarding "Violent Television Programming and Its Impact on Children," Federal Communications Commission, April 6, 2007. www.fcc.gov.

83. Marjorie Heins, "Politics of TV Violence Returns to Center Stage: FCC's TV-Violence Report," First Amendment Center, April 29, 2007. www.firstamendmentcenter.org.

List of Illustrations

How Does Media Violence Affect Society?

Violent Crime in the United States Has Decreased 33

Parents Believe Media Violence Harms Children 34

Exposure to Media Violence Increases Student Involvement
in Physical Fighting 35

Viewing Television Violence Increases the Likelihood of
Violent Behavior 36

Do Violent Video Games Inspire Violence?

Youth Video Game Playing Is Substantial 49

Much of Youth Video Game Playing Is Unsupervised 50

Violent Crime Is Decreasing as Video Game Violence Increases 51

Violent Video Games Increase Aggression 52

Is Current Regulation of Media Violence Effective?

Television Ratings Fail to Identify All Violent/Sexual Content 67

Majority of Video Games Are Appropriate for Youth 68

Most Music Videos Do Not Contain Violent Images 69

Incomplete Enforcement of Media Ratings 70

How Can the Problems Associated with Media Violence Be Reduced?

Violence on Television Has Increased 85

Majority of Parents Say They Monitor Children's Media Use 86

Limited Support for Increased Government Regulation 87

Most Parents Are Satisfied with Blocking Tools 88

Index

ACT Against Violence, 84
acts of violence
  in cartoons, 35
  simulated, youth viewing of, 8
  on TV
    numbers seen by children,
      11–12, 34
    per hour, 11
    trends in, 85 (chart)
    without punishment/
      condemnation for, 33
  types of, 12
aggression/violent behavior
  among children
    by level of exposure to violent
      TV, 36 (chart)
    media violence is not sole
      cause of, 82
  link between media violence
    and, 8, 24, 25, 28–32
    parents' views on, 34 (chart),
      35
  link between video games and,
    43–47, 48, 52 (chart)
American Academy of Child and
  Adolescent Psychiatry, 17, 46
American Academy of Pediatrics, 9
American Civil Liberties Union
  (ACLU), 16, 19, 29, 82
American Psychiatric Association,
  34
American Psychological
  Association, 8, 35
Anderson, Craig A., 30, 38,
  39–40, 45

Benedict XVI (pope), 83

Berg, Nick, 13
Be Web Aware, 65
Bickham, David, 30
Biskham, David, 58
Blanchard, Rashawn, 47
Brainwol, Mitch, 58
Buckleitner, Warren W., 64

Calvert, Clay, 77
Carnagey, Nicholas L., 30
Carter, Cynthia, 12, 27
Casal, Adolph, 40
Center for Digital Media
  Freedom, 41
children
  availability of violent video
    games to, 71
  average hours viewing TV by
    age 18, 11
  media violence as beneficial to,
    26–27, 31
  parents role in protecting from
    violent content, 73–74
  time spent on media among, 33
  video game playing among
    correlation with aggressive
      thoughts/behavior, 52, 52
      (table)
    parents' supervision of, 50
      (chart)
    prevalence of, 49 (chart)
  violent behavior in
    by level of exposure to violent
      TV, 36 (chart)
    link between media violence
      and, 8, 24, 25, 28–32
    parents' views on, 34

(chart), 35
media violence is not sole
cause of, 82
vulnerability to effects of media
violence, 9
vs. adults, 26
Christian Science Monitor
(newspaper), 74
Clinton, Hillary Rodham, 31, 53,
56, 59–60
COPA Commission, 57
Copps, Michael J., 72, 77, 81
crime/crime rate, 34, 43
media violence and, 25–26
trend in, 33 (chart)
correlation with introduction
of video games, 51 (chart)
See also aggression/violent
behavior

Department of Justice, U.S., 34

Edgar, Patricia, 31
Eekels, Pancho, 42
Entertainment Software
Association, 17
Entertainment Software Rating
Board (ESRB), 15
Eubanks, Janie, 30

Federal Communications
Commission (FCC), 10, 20, 82
on media violence and
aggressive behavior, 21
Federal Trade Commission (FTC),
65
Ferris, Duke, 37, 39, 43
First Amendment, 77
regulation of media violence
and, 19–20
Fredrickson, Caroline, 75, 82
Freedman, Jonathan L., 12, 23, 28

Free Expression Policy Project, 16,
23, 31

Gentile, Douglas A., 17, 46
Gerstein, Neil, 40, 45
government. *See* regulation, by
government
Grand Theft Auto (video game), 37
Graves, Joan, 54
Gross, Miriam, 12

Halliburton, Rachel, 12
Heins, Marjorie, 10, 26, 78
Hoppe, David, 14

Internet
music videos on, types/
frequency of violence on, 69
(chart)
violence in children's sites on, 66
violence on, 57
Ivie, George, 80

Jenkins, Henry, 14, 40
Jerk, Courtney, 30
Johnson, Marv, 75
Journal of Adolescence, 52
*Journal of Broadcasting and
Electronic Media,* 23
Journal of Young Investigators, 41

Kaiser Family Foundation, 11, 49,
84
Kids Rick Project, 66
Killian, Seth, 39, 45

Lee, Mickey Suhn, 41, 44
Los Angeles Times (newspaper), 80

Martin, Kevin, 81
McDowell, Robert M., 72, 76
McIntyre, Jeff, 24

McMasters, Paul K., 21
McSlarrow, Kyle, 19, 55, 62, 66
media
  society's use of, 11
  See also specific media
media violence
  debate over regulation of, 17–19
  effects of, 24–25
    beneficial, 16, 26–27, 31
    negative, 15–16
    research on, 22–23, 32
  First Amendment and
    regulation of, 19–20, 82, 83
  government regulation of,
    74–76, 77, 82
    opinion on, 84, 87 (chart)
  industry self-regulation of,
    14–15, 54–58, 59–60, 77–78
  overall level of, 73–74
  public opinion on, 54
  public perception vs. research
    definitions of, 23–24
  reasons for, 14
  trends in, 12–13
Moore, Robert, 62
Motion Picture Association of
  America (MPAA), 14, 54–55,
  61, 66
movie ratings, 14–15, 54–55
  effectiveness of, 62
music, violent lyrics in, 30
  effectiveness of, 57–58
  labeling for, 15
music videos, Internet, types/
  frequency of violence on, 69
  (chart)

National Institute on Media and
  the Family, 8, 11, 17, 26, 29,
  37, 50, 70, 76
National Youth Violence
  Prevention Resource Center, 33

Pandagon, Amanda, 80
parents
  agreement with video game
    ratings, 66
  monitoring children's media use,
    58–59, 68, 73–74
  opinion on, 84
  prevalence of, 86 (chart), 89
  restricting violent TV viewing,
    70
  satisfaction with TV blocking
    tools/ratings among, 88
    (chart), 89 (chart)
Pediatrics (journal), 32, 59, 70
Pew Research Center, 84
Policinski, Gene, 75
Potter, W. James, 10, 20, 29, 79

ratings
  media, inforcement of, 70
    (table)
  See also specific media
Recording Industry Association of
  America (RIAA), 15, 58
regulation, 9
  by government, 74–75, 82
    feasibility of, 75–76
    First Amendment and, 77
    opinion on, 84, 87 (chart)
    public opinion on, 78
  by industry, 14–15, 54–58,
    77–78
Rideout, Victoria, 64
Rosenbaum, James M., 44

Saunders, Kevin W., 16, 28
society, use of media in, 11
Solomon, David H., 53
Stone, Geoffrey R., 83
Suderman, Peter, 59
Sullum, Jacob, 81

Tate, Deborah Taylor, 56, 62, 80
Tearchers Resisting Unhealthy
  Children's Entertainment, 64
television
  average hours turned on, 10
  average hours viewed, by
    children, 11
  blocking tools, parents'
    satisfaction with, 88 (chart)
  ratings for, 55–56
    effectiveness of, 62, 66, 67
      (chart)
    parents' satisfaction with, 89
  violence on
    aggression and, 26 (chart)
    frequency of, 32, 84
    without punishment/
      condemnation for, 33
Thierer, Adam, 41, 56–57, 72
Thomson, Clive, 47
Thomson, Kim, 61

Valkenberg, Patti M., 44
Vance, Patricia E., 63
V-chip, 76, 81
video games

age appropriateness of, 68
  (chart)
benefits of, 41–42
link between violence and
  violent content in, 17, 43–47
  active participation and,
    39–40
  evidence against, 37
  evidence for, 38
  factors in, 40–41
ratings of, 8, 15, 56–57
  effectiveness of, 62–64, 71
sales of, 48
Violence in the Media (Carter and
  Weaver), 12
Viteritti, Joseph P., 27

Walsh, David, 11
Weaver, C. Kay, 12, 27
Webb, Theresa, 55
White, Daphne, 42
Winter, Tim, 79

Young, Shannon, 24, 29
youth violence. *See* aggression/
  violent behavior

About the Author

Andrea C. Nakaya, a native of New Zealand, holds a BA in English and an MA in communication from San Diego State University. She currently lives in Encinitas, California, with her husband, Jamie, and their daughter, Natalie. In her free time she enjoys traveling, reading, gardening, and snowboarding.